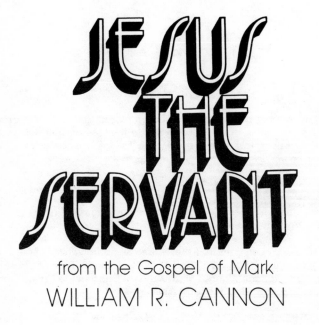

# JESUS THE SERVANT

from the Gospel of Mark

WILLIAM R. CANNON

THE UPPER ROOM

Nashville

JESUS THE SERVANT

Library of Congress Catalog 78-62578

Unless otherwise identified, all scripture quotations are from the King James Version of the Bible.

The scripture quotations from the Revised Standard Version of the Bible (RSV), copyright 1946, 1952 and © 1971 by the Division of Christian Education, National Council of Churches of Christ in the United States of America, are used by permission.

New Testament quotations from Today's English Version of the New Testament (TEV), copyright by American Bible Society 1966, © 1971, are used by permission.

First printing, June, 1978 (10)

ISBN 0-8358-0376-7

Printed in the United States of America

4

# CONTENTS

# FOREWORD

One of the most memorable experiences of my seminary days was a course in church history taught by the then dean of Candler School of Theology, William R. Cannon. The most unforgettable lecture in that memorable series was on Jesus. Dean Cannon left a class spellbound and in silence for five minutes following, as he climaxed his lecture with an emphasis on the incarnation and a recitation of Gilbert K. Chesterton's poem, "The House of Christmas."

I relived some of those high moments as I read this manuscript by my friend who is now a bishop of the United Methodist Church. Bishop Cannon is a brilliant scholar, a powerful preacher, a scintillating lecturer, and a convincing writer. He has combined these rare gifts to give us a helpful book on the Gospel of Mark.

As editor of *The Upper Room* I am committed to providing the most effective spiritual growth resources for our readers. A big part of that must be a devotional study of scripture. This book is in that category of devotional Bible study. It evokes a serious consideration of the person and work of Christ, calls

7

for a deeper commitment to him, enlightens, enlarges and enhances the reader's relationship to Christ.

It follows in the excellent tradition of Bishop Cannon's earlier study of the Gospel of Luke, published by The Upper Room, entitled, *A Disciple's Profile of Jesus.*

I commend it knowing that it will inspire, motivate and help others as it has helped me.

Maxie D. Dunnam
Editor, *The Upper Room*

# PREFACE

Activism is the chief characteristic of these times. With the possible exception of the Acts of the Apostles, Mark's Gospel is the most activistic book in the New Testament.

Activism as presented by Mark is quite different from most of the activism we witness in society today. Our activism polarizes and divides people. Everybody is interested in getting for himself/herself all that he/she can, and every group is pushing its own interest at the expense, and often to the detriment, of others.

Saint Mark presents Jesus as a servant. His activism is selfless, and everything he does is for the betterment of others.

The church needs to consider afresh her own form of activism and test it against the self-sacrifice of Jesus. Therefore, Mark's Gospel is more relevant today than ever before.

This little book is based on a series of talks I gave last February to the people of the Atlanta Area during the Bible Hour of Winter Camp Meeting at Epworth-by-the-Sea. Therefore, the book is written in a simple and direct manner and is offered as a piece of devotional literature. It does, I trust, represent adequate scholarship and research, but it is designed for the general public, especially the laity of the church.

William R. Cannon
Pentecost, 1978

### CHAPTER ONE

# THE SERVANT OF HIS PEOPLE
## (Mark 1:1–4:34)

### PURPOSE
(1:1)

*S*aint Mark tells his story in a brief manner, hurriedly, almost impatiently. His composition conveys the impression that this is a job he is compelled to do and one that he would like to complete as quickly as possible.

Certainly his is the shortest of the four Gospels. Because it is the shortest, many modern scholars assume that it is the earliest as well. The Gospels of Matthew and Luke appear to be expansions of Mark's Gospel. When Matthew and Luke wrote their Gospels, they must have had Mark's in front of them.

Tradition has it, however, that Matthew wrote his Gospel first. From the arrangement of the Gospels in our Bibles we might assume that he did. If so, Mark would be an abridgment of Matthew.

Mark's Gospel was written early enough to typify the transition from oral to written accounts of the words and works of Jesus. He moved from the spoken word to literary documents that would preserve for posterity the mighty message of Jesus of Nazareth. What had been seen and heard by actual eyewitnesses, and passed by word of mouth to countless others, would now in this short Gospel be the beginning of a corpus of literature that would become the New Testament. Why Mark was the first to write it down, perhaps nobody will ever know. It is possible that the Christian congregation to which he belonged required it of him. He was well qualified to write it. He is reported to have been the nephew of Barnabus. He was also the travelling companion of Barnabus and the Apostle Paul on their first missionary journey. Later, and above all else, he was the confidant of the Apostle Peter. Mark's Gospel is thought, therefore, to reflect Peter's own impression of his Lord and savior Jesus Christ. If so, his Gospel is of incomparable importance in the literature of Christianity.

The congregation for whom he wrote was the church at Rome, the capital of the Empire. Peter died during the persecution of Nero in A.D. 64. After this Mark evidently felt that he should write down for his Christian brethren what he had learned of Jesus from Peter; yet he was not wholly dependent on Peter. His own knowledge of Judea and Galilee and the times in which Jesus lived indicates that he himself was a Jew. Mark had lived, if not with Jesus himself, at least in the same surroundings and among the same people with whom our Lord had spent his life on earth.

Mark makes no effort, however, to reconstruct the life of Jesus. What he wrote bears little resemblance to either chronology or geography. He makes no effort to arrange his materials in historical sequence or to identify with any degree of exactness the places he mentions. It is enough for him just to say "wilderness," "sea," or "mountain." He denotes time merely with "it came to pass," or "it took place on the Sabbath," or "He went straightaway." What happened because of Jesus is dealt with in abundance. What happened to Jesus, himself, or the impressions made on Jesus by people and events, are scarcely dealt with at all. From Mark's Gospel we do not learn when Jesus was born, what he looked like, how long he lived, or very much else that provides color and concreteness to a human life. Mark's composition is not a biography. It is a presentation of the mighty acts of God as these acts are expressed in the deeds of Jesus of Nazareth. Mark is not interested in the person of Jesus but in what happened by the grace of God in and through the activity of Jesus. His work is not a biography but a gospel—God's good news for us in Jesus Christ. From beginning to end, Jesus is pictured as a servant of God. He is one who never does his own will but always the will of Him who sent him. The translation from the Greek of the word *son* can be "servant" as well. In Mark's case, "servant" is really a better and more accurate translation than "son."

The purpose of this Gospel is to demonstrate in mighty deeds and words God's salvation of humankind in Jesus Christ and to declare the same to all who believe. Hence the caption of the whole Gospel is its opening words, "the Good News of Jesus Christ, the Son (or servant) of God" (Mark 1:1, TEV). It is of the greatest importance to realize at the outset that this good news is not what Jesus reported and preached but what he demonstrated in his person on earth as the representative and the personification of God. Gospel is Good News about Jesus Christ.

## PREPARATION
(1:2-1:3)

Having declared in the opening words his purpose in writing, Saint Mark attempts to prepare his readers to understand and appropriate its contents in keeping with God's intention for their lives. As the servant of God, Jesus did not come for self-aggrandizement. He was not "out-for-himself." He came for persons and their salvation. His mission was to be the servant of his people.

Mark makes his readers privy to information and insights that were not available to the contemporaries of Jesus who took part in the fulfillment of his career. Not all the actors in the story of Jesus were aware of what was happening when the events in which they participated took place. Mark says that Jesus actually prevented them from comprehending the full significance of his words and deeds. They saw but did not perceive; they heard but did not understand.

Nonetheless, the readers of his Gospel will realize from the very outset what the story means. Since Mark was reared in a Jewish household, he was familiar with the expectations of his people and their hopes for deliverance through the intervention of

God. He explains that Jesus of Nazareth is the agent of that intervention, the fulfillment of those hopes, and the fulfillment of God's promise to his people in the Old Testament.

Mark uses a combination of verses from Isaiah 40 and Malachi 3 to introduce his story. The combination of these two Old Testament passages has led some scholars to assume that the primitive Christian community had already assembled in manuscript form all the passages in the Old Testament that referred to Jesus and that Mark used this compilation. No such book now exists. I know of no reference to it in the earliest literature of Christianity; so this, like so much else of modern biblical scholarship, is farfetched and fanciful. Mark paraphrases rather than quotes. This fact leads us to think that he had nothing before him and that he depended entirely on his memory.

Mark uses these passages only to show that the Messiah would have a forerunner. To do this, he has to lift the passages out of context; for their reference is to God himself, not to any earthly agent. Yet his method is no different from that of the rabbis. The Old Testament deals with the intervention of God in human affairs, and that is the major point. Whether that intervention is direct or indirect is of minor concern. Mark assumes that "the voice crying in the wilderness" is John the Baptist. He sees the mission of John as the evangelist sees it: It is to recognize and to declare the Messiah. Therefore we learn nothing whatever from Mark about John's mission, or even who John was and whence he came. John stands in

15

this Gospel solely as the forerunner of Jesus. Clothed in camel's hair and with a leather girdle around his waist, this man—who ate insects like the locust for meat, and wild honey for dessert—was just waiting for Jesus to come, so that he might recognize him and reveal him to others. In the meantime, of course, he did receive all those who went out to him and confessed their sins. He baptized them in the river Jordan. Mark exaggerates when he says those penitents consisted of all the people of Jerusalem and all the country of Judea. There were not that many. This is poetic license. Its intention is to convey to the readers that only a national repentance will be big enough to avoid judgment and prepare Israel for its Messiah.

According to Mark, John's role is to declare that his own baptism by water will be replaced by the baptism of Jesus with the Holy Spirit. The heavens, which had been closed to the people because of their sins, are now opened once again. The Spirit descends out of heaven as a dove, and God says, "This is my beloved Son, in whom I am well pleased" (Matthew 3:17).

As Mark employs John the Baptist to be the herald of Jesus, so does he use the devil to emphasize that Jesus is the Messiah. In two short verses Mark dispenses with the temptation of Jesus by the devil. He says that the Spirit forced Jesus into the wilderness, where he stayed forty days and was continually tempted by Satan. The word *tempted* can also be translated "tested." Mark shows in his account of the temptation that the Messiah must fight against all the evil forces in life. Jesus fights against the evil forces and prevails over them. Then, through his angels, God ministered to Jesus. The moral and psychological aspects of this experience, which come out in the later Gospels, are passed over by Mark without mention. They are not germane to his purpose, which is simply to declare the sufficiency of Jesus to deal with all evil and sin and to show his superiority over the devil.

Therefore both the mention of the baptism of Jesus by John the Baptist and the story of the temptation serve the same end. They are Mark's way of doing what Matthew and Luke do in their birth narratives and what John does in his Prologue. Each of these accounts complements and supports the others. They all give Jesus his divine credentials and establish the basis of his authority, identifying him as the Son of God.

## PRESENTATION
### (1:14-45)

The narrative of Jesus' ministry, as Saint Mark depicts it, begins with Jesus' entry into Galilee from the lower regions of the Jordan and the wilderness of Judea. Though Mark does not locate these places, he tells us that Jesus came into Galilee announcing the good news of the Kingdom of God. It is characteristic of Mark that Jesus always and invariably calls people to the opportunities and responsibilities of the

17

Kingdom. Jesus does not call people to allegiance to himself.

There are two requirements for appropriating the benefits Jesus offers. One is remedial: that they repent—that is, that they renounce what they now are, that they turn completely around and seek an entirely new personal orientation. *Repent* means much more than just an alteration of opinions. It means a change in the whole personality. The other requirement is positive: that they believe the good news which Jesus proclaims. Although there is nothing people can do to improve themselves, God can and will do everything for them, if only they will let him.

Jesus proceeds then to show what God can and will do, and this great demonstration is the way Mark presents Jesus in his Gospel. The forerunner of Jesus, John the Baptist, has completed his mission and is off the scene. The Greek text is more explicit than the English. Our text reads, "Now after that John was put in prison." But the literal Greek is, "after John was handed over." Since his work was finished, he was handed over to his enemies. Nothing could happen to him unless God permitted it to happen, and presumably this is what God was willing to do.

Jesus now stands alone, and the first thing he does in Galilee (his first messianic act) is to choose his four immediate disciples, Andrew, Peter, James, and John. They are chosen from those catching fish and are commissioned and empowered to catch people instead. "I will make you become fishers of men" (Mark 1:17b, RSV). Jesus' first act is evangelistic. If

18

proselytism is said to be at the heart of Judaism, so that every rabbi seeks to win as many disciples as he can, then evangelism is at the heart of Christianity. One must be a disciple before he can expect to become an apostle. It is the characteristic of Christian discipleship, even in its most rudimentary form, to win other disciples to the Master.

Jesus set up headquarters in Capernaum. Except for the priesthood in Jerusalem, the Jewish ministry was entirely a lay ministry. Anybody who could read the Old Testament lesson and had the mind to expound the same was eligible to preach in synagogues. Evidently Jesus spoke in the synagogue on this first Sabbath. Mark does not tell us what he said, but he is careful to tell us how he said it. Jesus spoke with authority, and not as the scribes. The scribes were bound, always, by precedent. They had to know and review everything that had ever been said about a text before they would offer their own opinion about its meaning—and this they did with hesitancy and trepidation. Jesus, in contrast, spoke with authority, for he said that he spoke in the name of God.

The essence of Jesus' message was never in words, but in deeds. When he saw a man in the synagogue with an unclean spirit, the unclean spirit inside the man recognized him and asked Jesus to leave him alone, saying, "Let us alone; what have we to do with thee, thou Jesus of Nazareth?" (1:24a) But Jesus did interfere, and the unclean spirit said, "Art thou come to destroy us? I know thee who thou art, the Holy One of God" (1:24b). "And Jesus rebuked him saying,

Hold thy peace, and come out of him" (Mark 1:25). The people could not fail to observe what had happened. They felt that Jesus had some new doctrine so that even the unclean spirits obeyed him. Later that day he cured Simon Peter's mother-in-law of fever. She immediately began to serve him and his friends, presumably at the evening meal. Saint Jerome says of this incident, that the human constitution is such that after pain our bodies are rather tired; but, when the Lord restores health, the restoration is immediate and complete.

The Jewish day lasted from sunset to sunset. Therefore the Jews in Capernaum who did not want to desecrate the Sabbath waited until sundown to bring their sick before Jesus to be healed. They presented him with all manner of diseases, both physical and mental, and he cured them all. As a result, he was tired. Nothing is quite so debilitating as being constantly in a crowd. He retreated before daybreak to pray. When his disciples found him to take him back, he did not return immediately but rather broadened the scope of his work by going to nearby villages and towns to help the people there. It was in one of those villages that a leper found him. The rabbis considered that it was as difficult to cure a leper as to raise a dead person from the grave. The disease was loathsome, infectious, disfiguring, and deadly. Lepers had to be separated from the rest of society; it was illegal even to touch a leper. So much were the people in dread of the disease that they took every known precaution to prevent its spread; yet Jesus touched and healed the leper who came to him. Then he sent him to the priests for examination and the official endorsement that he was well. Jesus cautioned the leper to tell no one how he had been cured. The leper utterly disregarded Jesus' request and told everybody the wonderful news of his cure and the name of Jesus, who had cured him.

As a result, Jesus was beset by a throng of people, so that he could not afford to go back into town. He stayed in the desert and received as many as came to him.

## HOSTILITY
### (2:1–3:6)

Saint Mark does not indicate that Jesus encountered any criticism or opposition for doing all the marvelous works he has described thus far. Everyone, it seems, was grateful, especially those for whom he performed his miracles. Those who came to him in the desert needed him and appreciated him; his critics stayed at home.

But when he came back to Capernaum, the situation was entirely different. Everybody in the region knew about him. Anyone who does anything of a public nature that puts himself in the public eye will sooner or later fall into the hands of critics. There seems to be nothing that wins universal approbation.

Saint Mark relates five incidents in which Jesus stirred up opposition and brought severe criticism on himself and his work. That these incidents are grouped together in Mark's Gospel does not necessarily mean that they happened in rapid succession, with each one following immediately upon the former. It could be that Mark arranged his material topically rather than chronologically. Mark may not have known exactly when each event occurred in the career of Jesus. After all, what he reports is what came either directly from the Apostle Peter or from persons in the congregations that Peter had served. It is not likely that Peter, who gave this information in conversations and sermons, would have put the incidents in historical order. Illustrations are used whenever needed in public discourse to make vivid and to confirm the point that is being emphasized. *Form criticism,* one of the modern scholarly techniques for understanding and interpreting the Gospels, views most of the sources as sermons or lessons. These would have been told time and time again to the emerging congregations of Christian believers. Naturally, the most prominent preachers to use such incidents were the apostles themselves. It was they who had been with Jesus. Since Mark was not an apostle, he had to depend on what he had heard either directly from them or from people to whom they had preached.

The last of these incidents took place in the synagogue on the Sabbath. Jesus healed a man whose hand was withered. Since it was not an emergency (evidently, the man had been in that condition since his birth), his critics wondered why Jesus did not wait until the first of the week to heal him. They thought there was no necessity for him to violate the Sabbath.

22

Mark explains, however, that in seeing the man's condition, Jesus called out to him, "Stand up!" Jesus wanted everybody to see what he was about to do. He healed him.

His response to his critics was, "Is it lawful to do good on the sabbath days, or to do evil? to save life, or to kill?" (Mark 3:4) He might have added, by way of explanation, that it is impossible to do nothing at all. He could have said, "It takes no more effort for me to heal this man than it does for you to criticize me for doing it. In your protesting what I have done, you are working just as hard as I am. Therefore, we are both violating the Sabbath; but I am doing it in a constructive, wholesome way, while your work is altogether negative and counterproductive." After he got through with them, they said nothing more in public about this incident.

This incident was preceded by another that also involved the Sabbath day. As Jesus and his disciples had walked through a field of grain, Jesus permitted them to pluck corn from the field and to eat it. They were hungry and the corn was readily available. They thereby violated the law of the harvest. People were forbidden to gather in their crops on the Sabbath day. Jesus responded to the critics by explaining that his disciples were not sent to harvest grain. They plucked just enough grain to satisfy their own hunger. David and his soldiers had done the same. In fact, they had even invaded the Tabernacle and eaten the consecrated bread that had been placed on the altar by the priests. This bread, the *shewbread,* was reserved for the priests. However, when people are in dire need anything that God has made can be requisitioned for their relief. All human institutions including the Sabbath are in the service of humanity. They have been designed solely for our good. God made them for us, not us for them. Then Jesus threw in the face of the Pharisees a familiar aphorism from their own rabbinical teachings: "The sabbath was made for man, and not man for the sabbath" (Mark 2:27b).

Just as Jesus disregarded the Jewish law regarding the Sabbath, so also was he indifferent to the practice of fasting. He contended that fasting is an act of penitence, an expression of self-disapproval, of anxiety and inner turmoil. Those who fast do so because of their sad disposition and disconsolate state. The disciples of John the Baptist fasted because the Messiah had not come; now that he is here the disciples of Jesus should eat and be merry, as guests at a wedding feast in the presence of the bridegroom. When fasting is no more than a ritualistic custom, it is useless. One's inner state should determine whether he/she fasts or not.

It is in connection with this lesson that our Lord cautions people about the danger of putting new wine into old wine bags or of sewing new cloth onto an old garment. As the new wine ages, it ferments and expands, and the old bags will burst, even as the shrinking of new cloth will tear the old garment to which it is sewn. It is not possible to graft the Kingdom of God onto an old human institution. Society is incapable of being patched up. The present sinful social order must be replaced by a new order designed by God.

These three incidents are preceded in Mark's Gospel by the one in which Jesus eats with publicans and sinners. For this, the Jewish religious leaders criticized him severely. They felt that these people, since they did not observe Jewish dietary regulations, were ritualistically unclean and would therefore contaminate any devout Jew who might eat with them. More than that, fellowship about the table during a meal indicated the strongest bonds of friendship between the participants. That Jesus would eat with publicans and sinners meant that he considered himself one of them. Evil is insidious. When we associate with evildoers, we soon adopt their ways and habits as our own. "Touch not this man," they said, "he consorts with publicans (greedy and corrupt tax collectors) and sinners!"

"Yes," said Jesus, "I associate with them because they need me the most. Just as a doctor is obligated by his profession to spend most of his time with sick people in order to treat them, so have I come to save sinners." Genuine goodness is immune to sin. The character of God is not blemished because he deals with the worst and most depraved of sinners. God's very nature disposes him to love sinners. He does not rest from his seeking after them.

This brings us back to the very first of these incidents that engendered the hostility of the Jewish religious leaders. Saint Mark puts it in the beginning of his account, but, because it is the climax of the lot, we have reserved it for the last. Four men lowered a paralytic down through the roof of a house in order that Jesus might heal him. In healing him, Jesus said, "Thy sins be forgiven thee" (Mark 2:5b). The Jewish critics thought that these words of Jesus were arrogant blasphemy. Jesus had appropriated to himself the prerogative of Almighty God. Only God can forgive sins. They did not understand that Jesus, the Son, was but exercising the will of the Father. Jesus forgave sins as God would, simply because he *was* God.

The cure of the paralytic is the climactic incident in disclosing who Jesus really is. The human is unmasked only to show clearly the divine. This man is able to perform the mighty acts of God not simply because God is with him but because he possesses the fullness of God's nature himself.

## DISCIPLES
(3:7–4:34)

Opposition is always difficult to manage, and open hostility is a shattering experience even to the strongest of persons. Though the criticism and abuse which his critics heaped on him were offset by the adulation and support of the general public, that support did not completely alleviate the pain the Master felt as a result of the work of his enemies. People now thronged into Galilee from all parts of Judea, and even from Idumea and Tyre and Sidon beyond the Jordan. Of course he healed them of their diseases and exorcised the unclean spirits within them. The crowds were pressing in on him. Everybody was trying to touch him. He had to get away.

Consequently, he left them entirely and sought refuge on a mountain with the Twelve. Mark, at this point in his account, gives the names of the twelve disciples. As ancient Israel was divided into twelve tribes, so Jesus' church, the new Israel of God, would have its twelve apostles. Some of them, like Peter and John, would become significant leaders of world dimension. Others, like James the son of Alphaeus, Thaddaeus, and Simon the Canaanite, would not rise above mediocrity and would soon sink into historical oblivion. Judas Iscariot would eventually betray Jesus.

But at this time Jesus trusted all of them and expected from them their best. On the mountaintop he ordained them and commissioned them to preach his gospel. He gave them his own power to cure sickness and to cast out devils. It was to them, likewise, that he explained the meaning of his wondrous works, promulgated his teachings, and entrusted the secrets of the Kingdom of God.

According to Mark, the meaning of what Jesus did and said was carefully concealed from the general public. The devils discerned it and were frightened by it, but Jesus threatened them and charged them to tell no one what they knew. Only to the disciples was he willing at this time to disclose the secrets of his mission. To be sure, he would say many things in the presence of the multitude, but he knew that they would not comprehend the meaning of his discourse.

27

His family, for example, could not understand his perseverance in the face of hostility and the objection of the religious leaders of the people. They felt that he had gone crazy, which meant in the psychology of that day that he himself was possessed of demons. But he showed how illogical such an attitude was. How could one who was possessed of a devil cast out devils? Satan's kingdom is united. It has to be united if it has any chance whatever for survival. It is stupid to think that Satan would work against himself, that he would injure himself and impair his own effectiveness. A robber cannot go into a man's house and steal his goods unless he conquers the man and ties him up. Jesus suggested that is what would have to happen to himself before any devil could possess him and rob him of his sanity and effectiveness. It is possible, he insisted, for a person to be forgiven of any sin, even the sin of blasphemy. That person must not sin against the Holy Ghost, but if he sins against the Holy Ghost he will never be forgiven and will be in danger of damnation. What is the sin against the Holy Ghost? Jesus does not say, but in the context of this writing we would surmise that sin against the Holy Ghost is stubborn unbelief. To prefer Satan rather than God, and to choose the things of the world over the values of the Kingdom of God would be sin against the Holy Ghost.

Thus Jesus does not respond to his mother and his brothers when they come to take him away from his mission and back home with them. When he is apprised of their presence, he merely points to the multitudes seated about him and says of them,

28

"Behold my mother and my brethren!" (Mark 3:34b) The unity among people that is based on their faith in God and their devoted service to God is stronger than family ties and filial affection. "For whosoever shall do the will of God, the same is my brother, and my sister, and mother" (Mark 3:35).

It was to the multitude gathered on the shore, while he stood in a boat out in the lake, that Jesus told the story of the sower who scattered seed on the ground. In the East during the first century the sower scattered the seed first, then he plowed the soil in which he had thrown it. In this case, some of the seed fell by the wayside and was eaten by the birds. Some fell onto the shallow soil that covered the limestone below; it sprang up quickly but was scorched almost immediately by the sun, for it had no rootage. Some seed fell among the thorns and was choked, so that it yielded no fruit. The rest fell on good soil and yielded an abundant crop.

Jesus explained the meaning of the story to the disciples when they were alone together. The sower is he who dispenses the Word of God. The persons to whom the Word is preached are the various soils. Satan is portrayed in the birds who devour the seed that falls by the wayside. The thin soil stands for those who are superficial. These persons will receive almost anything gladly but lacking depth they get tired of what they have and move quickly to something else. Likewise, the seed among the thorns represents those who let the cares and tribulations of the world distract them from the truth of the Word. Those who accept the Word of God and persevere to the end in keeping it are represented by the good soil.

This story is not a typical parable. It is unlike the stories of the good Samaritan and the prodigal son in Luke's Gospel. A parable is a story. The total impact of the parable illustrates a truth. The parable of the good Samaritan, for example, defines the meaning of *neighbor.* He who took care of the wounded man proved to be his neighbor. The parable is realistic. It is taken out of the everyday experiences of common life. There is nothing puzzling or mysterious about it. It is exactly what it appears to be. The man whom the thieves wounded, robbed, and left half dead does not represent anything or anybody other than the traveler himself. The good Samaritan does not portray God or Jesus. He is simply the neighbor to the Jew who fell among thieves. But the story of the sower and the seed is different. Each part of it represents something else. Until it is interpreted and explained, it remains a mystery, a riddle. One must discern what each aspect of it represents in order to comprehend its meaning. The story is typical of Mark. A parable for him is a puzzle. The general public cannot solve the parable puzzle. Its meaning is reserved for Jesus' very own, the chosen of the Lord, to whom he is pleased to disclose its truth. "Unto you it is given to know the mystery of the kingdom of God: but unto them that are without, all *these* things are done in parables: That seeing they may see, and not perceive; and hearing they may hear, and not understand" (Mark 4:11-12a).

Following immediately upon this story are three

aphorisms, or pithy sayings, of Jesus. The first is in the form of a question. Is a candle to be hid in a bucket or under a bed? No. It is to be set where it will give out light. But, according to Mark, Jesus does not apply this aphorism as he does in the Sermon on the Mount found in Matthew's Gospel. In Matthew, Jesus tells people not to hide their good works. Here he says that sooner or later everything that is hid will be discovered, all secrets will be disclosed. Therefore it behooves everyone to take notice of what is being said.

The second aphorism recommends discernment. We are admonished to evaluate what we hear and to act in accordance with the best. "With what measure ye mete, it shall be measured to you" (Mark 4:24b). But, here again, this is not applied by Mark in the same manner that Matthew applies it. Matthew interprets it in terms of what we do to others. The way we treat others will determine how we are treated. Mark limits it entirely to what happens within ourselves. The amount of good we appropriate from what we have will determine the extent of the benefit we receive.

The third aphorism is no more than a reinforcement of the second. The amount a man receives will determine the amount he will be given. If he is able to take in and assimilate a lot, he can expect more. If not, he can expect to lose what little he has.

The Kingdom of God, the gift of divine grace, is self-sufficient and always creative and productive. It is like seed which the farmer plants in the soil and leaves until it sprouts and becomes a full ear of corn.

That is what discipleship is when we entrust ourselves entirely to God. What happens to a few dedicated disciples will eventually encompass a multitude, for discipleship is contagious. Those whom the Lord commissions will win others. What looks now like a tiny group of people will one day become a mighty, universal organization bringing salvation to all. The Kingdom of God is like the tiniest of seeds which grow into the largest of trees. The whole world will be sheltered and protected by the Christian movement, which Jesus has begun through his disciples.

Jesus revealed these truths to those who were willing to follow him. God had sent him to be the servant of his people. Jesus was faithful in ministering to their every need.

CHAPTER ONE
## PERSONAL REFLECTION

1. In your own words, and out of your own experience, define the meaning of gospel or Good News.

2. Mark perceived the mission of John the Baptist to be one of recognizing and declaring the Messiah. Think of those persons in your life who have pointed you to Christ by their words and lives?

3. What does Mark tell us is meant by the command to "keep the sabbath"?

4. Consider the words, The Kingdom of God is like "the tinest of seeds"? What does this mean for your life?

5. In what ways, did Jesus become a servant for his people?

33

# THE SERVANT OF THE LORD
## (Mark 4:35–8:26)

### THE FIRST NATURE MIRACLE
#### (4:35-4:41)

**A**t this juncture in Saint Mark's Gospel, there is a decided shift in emphasis. Oddly enough, it takes place in the last section of the fourth chapter, where we find the account of a miracle terminating the second discourse of Jesus. Because this miracle is placed inside a chapter of unrelated material and because the following chapter is a continuation of miraculous events, we can note the artificiality of the division of the Bible into chapters. This anomaly is not peculiar to Mark. It runs through the whole of Scripture. In fact, Mark and the other authors had nothing at all to do with the arrangement of the Bible into chapters. This device was imposed at a later date by those who did not write the Scriptures. This was done to make the Bible easier to read and to make particular passages easier to find. For this we are grateful, but we would be even more grateful if these scribes and editorialists had been more careful in their work. Their chapter divisions often remind us of school children whose first essays show that they do not know either when to begin or to end a paragraph. Here is an egregious example: Mark's fourth chapter should end with verse 34 and the fifth chapter should begin with verse 35 of the fourth chapter.

The emphasis shifts from the portrayal of Jesus as the servant of his people to the portrayal of him as the servant of the Lord. I am aware that this distinction is a subtle one, but it is nonetheless essential if we are to understand the uniqueness of Mark's contribution. To be sure, it does not significantly change the nature of Jesus' work. He keeps on doing just as much good to people as he ever did. He is still their servant. Whereas heretofore he had appeared to be no more than the servant of his people, now, gradually disclosed is the revelation that what is happening in their behalf is of such a nature that God himself must be taking a personal interest in it. Jesus has at his disposal more resources than any ordinary teacher would have. We get a preview of this in the account of the healing of the paralytic, when Jesus forgave him his sins. This was an act that only God could do (Mark 2:5). But then, as a concession to his critics, he added the admonition to the healed man: "Rise, take up your pallet and go home" (Mark 2:11, rsv). More than this, Mark shows that Jesus is acting, step-by-step, in the fulfillment of a definite plan. That plan is God's plan for the salvation of his people.

It is one thing to observe someone in trouble and to go at once to his relief; it is quite another to set up a grand strategy for human deliverance and to carry it out with unrelenting determination. Until now, Jesus had brought relief to diseased and devil-possessed

35

individuals in Galilee. Now, says Mark, the disclosure is made that Jesus came into the world for the deliverance of humankind.

He begins this section of his Gospel, therefore, with the account of Jesus' first nature miracle, an entirely different kind of miracle from any he had performed. This man who can cure the human body of disease is able, also, to curtail and regulate the forces of nature.

Here Jesus imitates God precisely. The rabbis had taught that God made the world by bringing order out of chaos. The Jews from time immemorial had been impressed by the sea. Its violent storms, its tempestuous waves, and its shattering power depicted in their minds disorder, chaos, and evil. Therefore, the ability of anyone to still the waves and abate the storm was considered by them evidence of divine power. Only God could afford to disregard a storm, for only God knew himself to be more powerful than the storm and beyond its harm. If a human being could be calm in a storm, then he must believe in his heart that God will protect him and deliver him safely out of the storm. He not only has confidence in God's ability to curtail the storm, but he also trusts God completely to look after him.

It might be expected that Jesus would exemplify supreme confidence in God. Indeed, he did, for the rocking of the boat by the waves only intensified his sleep. He did not wake up. Even the filling of the boat with water about his reclining form did not seem to disturb him in the least. In contrast, the disciples, were terribly frightened. They woke him, fearful that both he and they would sink into the sea.

The real demonstration of the difference between a good man who trusted God for deliverance and a Savior who effected the deliverance of others is seen in what Jesus did. He did not say anything whatever to the disciples when they woke him. Instead, he turned to the sea and rebuked it. It was only after the sea calmed down, after the boat was steadied, and after its passengers were safe that Jesus said anything to his frightened companions. Then he asked, "Why are you afraid? Don't you have any faith?"

At this juncture, Saint Mark makes his crucial point. He tells us that the disciples looked at one another in awe and wonder: "Who then is this," they exclaimed, "that even the wind and the sea obey him?"

## A MIRACLE FOR A GENTILE
### (5:1-20)

Saint Mark follows the nature miracle with another healing miracle. This time, however, the miracle is not performed on one of Jesus' own people but on a gentile.

Jesus and his disciples cross the Sea of Galilee and land on the shore of the country of the Gadarenes. It is at once apparent that this is not Jewish territory, for there is a large herd of swine on the land near the shore. Even today this area is not in the land of Israel. It belongs to Syria. One can stand at the harbor of ruined Capernaum and see it just a short distance hence. (Anywhere one sails on the Sea of Galilee, it is but a short distance hence.) Jesus did not need to land there. He could just as conveniently have landed elsewhere. The sea was calm after the storm, the little boat was under control, his disciples were competent navigators. Jesus chose deliberately to land in this place.

Until now, he had performed the mighty acts of God on God's own people, the Jews. He had chosen as the scene of his activity his own land of Galilee, where he had grown up. At this point, he shifts both the scene of his mission and even the people toward whom it is directed. He goes to a foreign territory and performs a miracle for a foreigner. What more convincing evidence can we find to demonstrate that Jesus is now disclosing himself as the servant of the Lord, and the Lord as the God of the entire earth and all its peoples?

Mark tells us that when Jesus disembarked he was immediately accosted by a crazy man whose insanity was of such a violent variety that he cast himself against the sharp rocks of the caves where he resided. He had no disposition to be with people, and people tried to avoid him. He was dangerous. They did not know what he might do to them. The natural impulse of anyone on seeing him would be to get away as fast as he possibly could. Jesus' natural impulse would have been to jump back in the boat and have his disciples turn out to sea again.

The crazy man recognized Jesus from afar. He ran to the point of his landing and worshipped him. Yet, at the same moment that he fell down at the feet of the Master in awe and adoration, he pleaded with him to go away and leave him alone. He claimed to have nothing in common with Jesus. This was strange conduct. It shows how crazy the man was.

Here is a typical case of schizophrenia, a divided personality. The poor man wants to receive Jesus and to be rid of him at the same time. The devil in him cries out, "What have I to do with thee, Jesus, *thou* Son of the most high God? I adjure thee by God, that thou torment me not" (Mark 5:7). You will notice that throughout Mark's Gospel the devils always recognize Jesus. They know who he is and what he is about, even when the general public and Jesus' own followers do not. The devils recognize Jesus as their enemy. Either they must destroy him or he will destroy them. Saint Mark is bent on showing his readers the intense struggle God is waging with Satan, the fight that is going on between good and evil.

If this is the case, why is Jesus so indulgent with the demon? He asks the demon his name, only to be told that the name is legion, because there is not one demon but innumerable demons in the man. The spokesman for these demons pleads with Jesus that he not send them out of the country but rather allow them to enter the herd of swine feeding near the mountain. Oddly enough, Jesus honors their request.

Since the man who was inhabited by these demons was a gentile, they adapted themselves to gentile thoughts and manners. We may style them *gentile demons.* They used the Roman vocabulary to identify themselves. Their name was *legion.* A

Roman legion consisted of six thousand soldiers. Evidently there were six thousand demons in that one poor man.

Mark tells us that there were three thousand pigs in the herd nearby. When Jesus permitted the demons to enter the pigs—if they divided themselves equally among the swine—there was one pig for every two demons.

Jesus accommodated the demons by honoring their request and permitting them to enter the swine. But this accommodation was only a temporary one. The frightened pigs ran out into the sea and were drowned. Evidently the demons were drowned with them. Jesus had not signed a truce with evil. His opposition to it was complete.

The Gadarene people who had lost so many pigs were not at all happy about the incident. To be sure, the man who, when mad, had been so violent and strong that they could not restrain him, even with the stoutest of ropes, was now back in his right mind and would be a productive citizen again. Nonetheless, the people were frightened by such a display of power. They were displeased over their staggering financial loss as well. Rather than solicit the support of Jesus and harness his miraculous power for their benefit and salvation, they asked him to leave their country.

The healed man, grateful to Jesus for what he had done, asked to be made a part of Jesus' company and be allowed to go with him wherever he went with the other disciples. But Jesus refused. He knew that a gentile would be useless in Jewish territory. He would imperil the work and impair its effectiveness. Jews did not respect the gentiles. What could a gentile teach them about religion?

The man could be useful, however, among his own people—and, indeed, he was. He went about through the Roman area of the Decapolis testifying to Jesus and his miraculous power.

Therefore, the very first missionary to the gentiles was not Saint Paul. The first missionary was this Gadarene demoniac whom Jesus had restored to his right mind.

## CHRONIC ILLNESS AND DEATH
### (5:21-43)

Saint Mark does a most unusual thing in the next two incidents he describes. He starts out on one venture, interrupts it with another, and then goes back to conclude the venture with which he began. This has puzzled various commentators and scholars who have written on Mark. They have advanced all sorts of strange and curious reasons why Mark has done this. This interruption of one miracle by another is a unique occurrence in the Gospels. These scholars, with all their strange and complex reasons, have missed the one obvious and undebatable reason why Mark tells it as he does. The reason is that this is the way it happened.

While Jesus was on his way with Jairus to give his attention to his desperately ill daughter, Jesus was accosted by a woman in the crowd. Jesus had to heal her before he could go on. Everyone is interrupted from time to time in the performance of one duty by the urgency of another. We have to take care of the interruption. Telephone calls are a clear and constant example. Why is it that we must always answer the phone, no matter what else we may be doing?

A very important man, the ruler of his local synagogue, came to ask Jesus' help with his daughter. In this instance, "ruler of the synagogue" probably does not mean the person who arranged Sabbath worship on a regular basis; instead, it no doubt means the most wealthy, influential, and powerful person in that synagogue. Between the point where Jesus landed and his arrival at Jairus's house, his company grew into a big crowd of people.

There was a poor woman apart from the crowd, looking on. She was ceremonially unclean, because the Jews believed that women were unclean at the time of menstruation. They had to wait until that monthly process had ended before they were free to mix and mingle with people again. Otherwise, they would contaminate all with whom they associated.

This woman, however, had an internal condition that made her unclean all the time. She suffered from a continuous hemorrhage. She had exhausted every possibility for cure. She had consulted all the doctors she knew, and none of them had been able to help her. In addition to her illness, she was ostracized, forbidden by ancient Jewish law to have any contact with others.

Here was her one opportunity. She would throw herself unrecognized into the crowd and push her way through until she got to Jesus. "If only I can touch him," she thought, "he will be able to cure me."

She did touch Jesus. Immediately power went out from him and she was cured. The disciples were amazed when Jesus asked who touched him. In such a throng, not to be touched was impossible. But our Lord felt instantly the woman's need, and he knew that he had cured her. Here is another demonstration of the wonderful works of God. In performing this miracle Jesus showed clearly that he was acting as the servant of the Lord. The woman knew that being in the presence of Jesus was enough to satisfy her. His presence was just as powerful and wonder-working as the presence of God himself.

News came to Jairus that it was now too late. There was no need for him to trouble Jesus further. His little daughter was dead. But Jesus went on anyway. He told the father not to give in to his grief but to believe in God. When Jesus got there, the mourners had already begun to gather. There was a tumult about the house.

Jesus told the crowd that its demonstration of grief was premature. He said that the little girl was just sleeping. They all laughed in his face. Nevertheless, he took the child by the hand and said one hope-fulfilling word, the meaning of which was, "Damsel, I say unto thee, arise" (Mark 5:41b). And the little girl got out of bed and walked. Jesus ended his visit by telling the parents to prepare something for the child to eat.

In this incident, Jesus raised someone from the dead. Being God's servant, he can restore life. The same power that created life in the beginning can sustain and redeem that life, even from death.

## RESPONSE AND RESPONSIBILITY
(6:1-56)

The sixth chapter of Mark is long and disparate. It seems to hop, skip, and jump, with one apparently unrelated incident following another. There appears to be no pattern to it at all. When one looks at it more carefully, however, this is not the case. Stylistically, Mark's entire Gospel is rough-hewn; yet he is an artist whose care is evident in all that he does.

The burden of the sixth chapter is to show various responses to Jesus. At the same time, it deals with certain responsibilities that Jesus himself assumed in relation both to those responses and to the totality of his ministry as the servant of the Most High.

Saint Mark begins this section of his Gospel by telling us that Jesus returned to his own country. This is deceiving. Except for the visit to the country of the Gadarenes, he had been in his own country all the time. His entire ministry had been spent thus far in Galilee. When one examines the Greek text, this perplexity is at once relieved. In Greek the word which has been translated "country" means "city" as well. The opening verse of the sixth chapter should read, "And he went out from thence, and came into his own city." It was in Nazareth, the place of his birth, that the first incident occurred.

The people there were impressed by what he said

44

and did. Their evaluation of his ministry was just as high and just as praiseworthy as it had been everywhere else. Seemingly, there was no lack in their powers of discernment and judgment (Mark 6:2b). Nonetheless, they did not believe in him. The reason for their unbelief is apparent. They confused his background with himself and his message. His family were common laborers, and the people knew every one of his brothers and what each of them did. They knew his sisters, who still resided in the town, and they knew the widow, Mary, his mother. They even remembered when he himself worked as a carpenter among them and did menial work for them. Why should they believe in him? He did not have the right background. It was arrogant and presumptuous of him to try to teach them.

As an aside, Mark has Jesus identified as Mary's son (Mark 6:3a). This was a departure from Jewish custom, for Jews always identified a person by naming his father. Theirs was a male-oriented society. If Mark is quoting the people, as, indeed, he would have us believe, they must have done this in derision: "Here is mama's boy! He has come back again—this time as a teacher! He never was any good as a carpenter anyway!" Or Mark could have let slip his own personal knowledge. Without thinking, he could have attributed to the people of Nazareth only what real believers could have known, that Joseph was not Jesus' father. Jesus was the Son of God.

Our Lord, no doubt, was keenly disappointed by the response he got in Nazareth. He said simply, "A prophet is not without honor but in his own town and among his own kin and in his own house." The cynic Montaigne said centuries later that a great man is never great either to his wife or to his valet.

Jesus could not rely on his own family for help. He had to depend on his disciples. Whereas they had heretofore exercised their discipleship by staying close to him, he now realized that he must send them out on their own. So he sent them out, two together. He told them what to take—very little! They were to take only what they needed. He told them what to do—they were to do exactly what Jesus himself did. They had been with him and had seen him. They were to imitate him, by healing the sick, by casting out devils, and by preaching so that people should repent. He told them, also, how to behave. They should graciously accept the hospitality of any who received them, but in places where they were not well received they should shake the dust from their feet. This was a thing Jews always did when they came home from gentile territory. They did not want to bring the contaminated soil of an unclean land into their own holy land. By this sign the disciples would show unbelieving Jews what they thought of them. By not believing in Jesus they were worse than the citizens of Sodom and Gomorrah.

When Herod heard what was happening in his country of Galilee, he was disturbed, actually frightened, for he thought that John the Baptist had come alive again. Herod ruled Galilee as an agent of Rome. He had had John the Baptist beheaded at the request of Herodias, whom John had condemned along with Herod because of their marriage. Herodias had been married to Herod's half-brother whom she divorced to marry Herod. John the Baptist did not approve of that divorce and remarriage, and he was fierce in his attack on it, as he was on all evil. Salome, Herodias's daughter by her first marriage, pleased Herod by her dancing and won his oath that he would give her anything she asked of him. He made his oath in public. Therefore, when her mother told her to ask for the head of John, Herod could not refuse his step-daughter without losing face.

Mark inserts this story. The death of John had happened earlier. Mark uses it to indicate Herod's reaction to Jesus. It is unique. It is the only incident Mark records in his entire Gospel that does not deal directly with Jesus himself.

The disciples return and give Jesus a report on their mission. He then invites them to go away with him into the desert. But the people also follow—five thousand of them. After they had listened to the Master all day, he does not want to send them away famished and weak. He feels that it is his responsibility to give them food as well as instruction. Therefore, he multiplies five loaves of bread and two fish, so that five thousand people are amply fed. Modern exegetes tend to see in this a prefiguring of the eucharist, a symbolic meal representing the messianic banquet of all true followers in the Kingdom of God. However, this is reading into the incident much that is simply not there. Jesus knew that the people were hungry. They needed food, and he provided what they needed. That is all there is to it. Jesus clearly taught that we cannot live by bread alone, but he knew that we cannot live without bread either. Jesus was a practical person, and he ministered to the whole of life.

Jesus sent the disciples ahead of him by boat to Bethsaida. In the night a storm arose and Jesus saw them on the sea, rowing hard, struggling against the waves. He walked out to them on the water. They thought what they saw was a ghost, but the sea became calm. Not until they reached shore in Gennesaret did they realize that it was Jesus whom they had seen walking on the water.

The news spread. The mighty agent of God was in Gennesaret. People ran about collecting all their sick and bringing them on cots to Jesus. The mere touch of the Master was sufficient: "As many as touched him were made whole" (Mark 6:56b). The picture of villages and towns with the sick laid out on the streets awaiting the coming of Jesus is a moving spectacle. The inanimate forces of nature may obey him, but only human beings can knowingly and openly respond to God.

## REBUKE
(7:1-23)

Jesus' teaching was not always positive. It was often negative. Rather than being put in the form of moral incentives and exhortations to goodness, it came in thunderclaps of rebuke and condemnation.

This was generally the case when he had anything to say to the scribes and Pharisees.

They complained that Jesus' disciples did not observe the ceremonial ritual of the Jews. For example, they did not always wash their hands before a meal. In their neglect they violated the tradition of the elders.

But what precisely was the tradition of the elders? The Law, so sacred to the Jews, was the law of Moses. It was preserved in written form in the Pentateuch. In addition to the law of Moses, there were the innumerable interpretations of it by rabbis and scribes throughout the centuries. These interpretations, though oral to begin with, were gradually reduced to written form. In Jesus' day there was no collection of them such as the Mishna and the two Talmudic forms. The Mishna is second century, while the two Talmuds are fifth and sixth century, respectively. According to them, the washing of hands was required only of the priests.

However, there is evidence that the strict rabbis in Jesus' time insisted, as Mark indicates, that all pious Jews observe it. The Pharisees then expected Jesus to require of his disciples the very highest standards of religious observance. "If Jesus is really the marvelous and convincing prophet the general public claims him to be," they reasoned, "can we expect anything less of him than the very best?" Such public protestations on their part were sarcastic, of course. Jesus was always the object of ridicule to them. The Sadducees, in contrast to the Pharisees, did not accept the oral tradition—but the Sadducees had little influence with the people.

Yet Jesus takes the position of the Sadducees at this point. He says that the oral tradition is of little value at best. At worst it is a subterfuge for the Law itself and an excuse for violating it. For example, on the pretext of taking an oath to support the Temple, some Jews neglect their parents, protesting that the money they would normally expend on them has been set aside for the worship of God.

Jesus teaches that what goes into a person, like food—kosher food to be exact—is inconsequential. It is what comes out of a person that really counts. Thoughts determine action. The things we conceive in our minds and cherish in our hearts set the style of our behavior and determine the quality of person we really are. Then, like Moses in the Ten Commandments, Jesus lists the specific sins we are constantly to guard against and always to avoid (Mark 6:21-22).

### HELP FOR THE GENTILES
(7:24–8:9)

Mark is very careful at this juncture to record that Jesus went into territory occupied by a considerable number of gentiles. There were Jews there, too, but the point the evangelist wants to make is that Jesus received the gentiles and helped them. He left Galilee and went into the lands of Tyre and Sidon.

On this venture Jesus does not seek out any gentiles. He does not advertise himself as available to them. Rather he goes inside a home, presumably a Jewish residence, probably to shut himself off for a few days. He was anxious that no one know precisely where he was.

But one woman found out. Maybe it was feminine intuition that led her to the place. She was an anxious mother seeking relief for her sick child. The distinctive characteristic that set this woman apart from all the rest was that she was a Greek. We saw earlier that Jesus had healed the Gadarene demoniac. He was not a Jew either. We called him a gentile to distinguish him from the Jews. But he was no doubt a Semite. Jesus came over to him as if to seek him out. In this instance, however, the mother tried to seek Jesus out. More than that, she had to persuade him to help her, for he seemed reluctant. His mission was to the Israelites. She was a Greek, a Syro-Phoenician woman.

Jesus used exaggerated oriental hyperbole in his conversation with her. He said that he had been sent to feed children (the Hebrews were thought of as the children of God), not dogs (the gentiles). She was desperate, so she could not afford to take offense. Humbly she replied, "Yet even the dogs are allowed to eat of the children's crumbs." She knew and he knew that every little child likes to give leftovers to his puppies. Jesus relented. "Because you have said what you did," Jesus replied, "you can go home with an easy mind. The devil has left your little girl."

This is the only instance in the Gospel where Jesus heals by long distance. He does not see the child. He does not require a description of her or the symptoms of her disease. Yet he exorcises her of the devil. When the mother reaches home she finds that her daughter is well.

Jesus came to the region of the Decapolis, presumably already evangelized by the Gadarene demoniac whom he had healed. There he is presented with a deaf person who has also an impediment of speech. He takes him aside, puts his fingers in his ears, and spits in his mouth and touches his tongue. After that he lifts his face heavenward and utters one word, and the man is healed. He hears clearly and speaks distinctly. Despite Jesus' request for secrecy, the news of the event is published everywhere.

Multitudes of people followed Jesus and hung onto his every word. Indeed, the crowd had been with him three days. There were four thousand of them. And our Lord fed them just as he did the five thousand in Galilee. The Galilean crowd had been Jewish. This crowd in the region of the Decapolis was gentile. He used five loaves on the first lot, symbolizing the five books of the Law. He used seven loaves on the second lot, symbolizing the seventy nations in which antiquity divided the gentile world. There were twelve baskets left over after the first feeding, representing the twelve tribes of Israel. There were seven after the second. Oddly enough, Mark uses two different Greek words for "basket" in the two feedings. The first means a Jewish type of basket; the second means an ordinary basket, one generally used for fish.

In this short section of his Gospel, Mark has

established his case: Jesus belongs to the gentiles as well as to the Jews. His mission is to all humanity.

## RIDDLES AND RELIEF
### (8:10-26)

He is accosted once again by the Pharisees, who demand a sign of him from heaven to attest to his trustworthiness and the validity of his work. He gives them nothing but disdain. Mark says that he walked away from them and took ship again upon the Sea of Galilee.

Aboard ship, a most peculiar incident occurred. The disciples became anxious that they had only one loaf of bread on board with them. What would they do when they all got hungry? Jesus told them to beware of the leaven of Herod and of the Pharisees.

It was obvious that the disciples did not know what Jesus meant by "the leaven of Herod and the Pharisees." They thought that it had something to do with their complaint that they had an insufficient supply of bread.

What he meant was that they, like Herod and the Pharisees, were interested in the wrong things. The leaven of Herod was his authority and power, the favor that the Romans conferred on him, enabling him to rule. The leaven of the Pharisees was the admiration—even the adulation—of the people, that gave them influence and enabled them to manipulate the crowds.

How needless was the anxiety of the disciples! The

Maker of bread was among them. They had forgotten, so soon, the miracles of the loaves and fishes. They had failed to discern in Jesus the power of Almighty God.

When they came to Bethsaida there was remaining yet another miracle for Jesus to perform. The people brought a blind man to him and begged him to restore his sight. He took the blind man out of town, spat in his eyes, and put his hands on him. When he asked the blind man what he saw, he replied, "I see people moving, but they look like trees." Jesus put his hands once again on the man's eyes, and what he saw as a result was clear and distinct.

This is a most peculiar incident. Its peculiarity lies in the fact that Jesus' first attempt at curing the man was only partially successful. There were results, to be sure, but these results were imperfect. It was like a cataract operation before a new lens is put in the eye. The patient sees, but indistinctly. In none of the other healing miracles did this happen. Why did it have to happen here? Our Lord's healing power is not like that of a physician, whose success or failure with his patient depends on his own skill and the responsiveness of the patient to treatment. How often we have heard that the operation was a success, but the patient's condition was so weak he died. The healing of diseases by physicians is seldom instantaneous. Healing is generally a gradual process.

Jesus effected cures immediately. His was not an acquired skill but a native endowment. The worse the patient's condition, the more readily our Lord cured him.

Why the second attempt? It was to show the man himself the difference between ordinary vision and the perfect vision of God. Most of us have natural sight. We can see how to get around to perform ordinary tasks, but it is that second touch that really enables us to see. We do not see as God intends us to see until we receive his own vision.

CHAPTER TWO
## PERSONAL REFLECTION

1. What did the first miracle described in this chapter reveal about who Jesus was and how others saw him?

2. What lesson does the healing of the possessed gentile have for us in our own time?

3. What does it mean to you that God both creates and restores life?

4. Jesus interpreted the Law of Moses in a new way for his own day. What does Jesus' new interpretation mean to you?

5. Reflect on the interactions between Jesus and other persons described in this chapter. Note particularly their differing responses to him and his words and actions. What guidance do you find for your own relationships?

### CHAPTER THREE

# THE MESSIANIC SERVANT
(Mark 8:27–10:52)

## PETER'S CONFESSION
(8:27-33)

**P**eter's confession is the "hinge" passage in Saint Mark's gospel. It enables the door of understanding—heretofore kept closed, except, perhaps, for a slight crack now and again—to be swung wide open, so that the nature of our Lord's mission is fully disclosed. The word *cardinal* in Latin means "hinge." The Roman Catholic Church designates those prelates next in rank to the Pope as cardinals. It is they who choose a new Pope when the reigning Pope dies. They are the princes of the church, the hinges on the door of the church, as it swings open to let people move from the present to the future. We may call this brief passage the cardinal section of Saint Mark's Gospel. On the basis of this passage the followers of Jesus move from questions and perplexities to clear answers.

Yet the right answers to the questions do not come as easily and as readily as one might expect. Christian understanding is a profound and complex process of learning. It takes place by stages. The longer one is with the Lord, the more one learns about him, and appreciates and trusts him.

The healing of the blind man is Saint Mark's transitional episode from one main division of his Gospel to another, from the recounting of incidents displaying the work of Jesus as the servant of God to their interpretation wherein we behold him as the true Messiah. Therefore, this section in Mark's Gospel presents us with the unfolding picture of the Messianic Servant. The servant motif is constant in Mark. It is there from start to finish. But the role of the servant varies, and we can see and appreciate the development of his ministry as the Gospel progresses.

The emphasis here is on "unfolding." The picture of Christ comes to the disciples only in partial, incomplete glimpses. That is why the miracle of the restoration of sight to the blind man at the end of the last section is so important for the understanding of this section. At first, he saw objects moving like trees. They all looked alike. Later, he beheld them exactly as they were, each in its own individuality and uniqueness.

Speaking for the group, Peter makes at the outset the right confession as to who Jesus is. But the content of that confession, the full delineation of Jesus' personality and behavior, is not perceived by him at once. Indeed, it is never adequately perceived until after the resurrection. Though the disciples at the time of Peter's confession know that the full nature of our Lord's mission is to bring deliverance and salvation, as God's Messiah, they are as ignorant as ever about how he will do it and what form his deliverance will take.

It was inevitable that everybody who had any contact with Jesus, or who had even heard about the things that he was doing, would form an opinion about him. Public opinion is formed out of all that goes on in public life, and everybody who deals with the public is interested in what it is. Jesus was no exception; so, as he and his disciples were travelling about in gentile territory, he asked them what the people were saying about him. We know—if not from the question, then at least from the answer—that it was not so much the gentile audiences that he had in mind, but the Jewish. After all, it was to the Jews—especially to those in the region of Galilee where he had been reared—that he had given most of his attention.

The answer he got from his disciples was most favorable. He was told that the people thought that he was John the Baptist, Elijah, or one of the prophets. This was a good answer; but it was not good enough. John the Baptist was a great and good man, but he was only a forerunner. The one he ran before would be far greater than he. Elijah marked only the beginning of prophecy. He did not represent it in the fullness of its development. He, too, was the Old Testament prototype of the herald of the Messiah. He was never thought to typify the Messiah himself. Hence, Jesus passed the answers by summarily.

He asked the disciples what they themselves

thought about him. "Who am I to you?" he asked. The *you* in Greek denotes a decided emphasis, meaning, "It is not important what these think about me. All that really matters is what you think!"

When Peter gave his answer—the right answer, at that—Jesus, according to Mark, does not dwell on it. He does not even bother to thank him for his evaluation or to commend him on the correctness of it. He does accept it, albeit tacitly. "Well, don't tell anybody about it," he says, as if to say, "Let them discover it for themselves."

Confession of faith in Jesus Christ is a highly personal affair. Nobody can confess him for anybody else. Though Peter presumably spoke for his colleagues as well as for himself, what he said did not count for them until they, each one, made Peter's confession their very own. The only way the church can make her confession of faith is on the lips and in the hearts of all her believing members. When her members do this, then her faith is vital and contagious. When they fail to do this, or err in their confession, then the church herself is brought thereby into apostasy. The church ceases to be her true self.

Jesus went on to explain to the group, "You know what this confession means. It means that the Messiah must suffer and die. Your expression of confidence in my life and work is also an expression of confidence in my death."

Now Peter had not meant to go this far. Rejection and execution as a criminal were not in his idea of messiahship at all. He thought of the Messiah as "great David's greater son." David had been the greatest military leader and conqueror in all Israelite history. He had put down all his enemies and had transformed the weak confederation of Jewish tribes in their new land into a united and invincible kingdom. If the Messiah was to be like David, then he would come as a conquering deliverer. He would put all the enemies of God and God's Kingdom under his feet. That was Peter's opinion, and Peter was not timid in expressing his opinion. Mark tells us that he led Jesus aside and rebuked him.

But observe the reaction of the other disciples, as Peter expostulated with Jesus on the subject. "He is right," they said. "Peter is right, Master. You know it. He has Scripture on his side." None of them was prepared to accept the other idea of messiahship; for, if the Master had to suffer and die, they realized that they, too, must suffer and die. When they became disciples of Jesus, they did not have this in mind. They expected to gain for themselves principalities and powers, kingdoms and dominions—not suffering and death.

Peter almost certainly discussed the issue with Jesus, in the company of his colleagues. He led Jesus aside only when he administered the rebuke to him. The discussion was in their presence, for Jesus brought Peter back to them to permit them to hear what he had to say to Peter. After all, what applied in this instance to Peter applied to them. "Get thee behind me, Satan" (Mark 8:33b), is what Jesus said. Jesus called Peter the devil—and by implication all the others were devils, too. Indeed, we are all devils when we substitute, as Peter did, the standards of this world for the standards of the Kingdom of God. Too many of us who call ourselves Christian still behave like Peter. We do not savor the things of God because we still savor the things of this world.

## SELF-DENIAL AND SELF-SACRIFICE
### (8:34-9:1)

The realization of self-denial and self-sacrifice was so important that Jesus carried his disciples out to the people, and to them he directed a discourse on self-denial and self-sacrifice. This is one of the most significant entries in Mark's Gospel, for it is crucial to the new religion which Jesus is establishing.

Jesus does not mince words. To be sure, what he says, as Mark reveals it, is always in abbreviated form. Nonetheless, even if he had employed the adornment of language and the courtesy of expression so characteristic of oriental speech, he could not have softened his message to such a degree that people would have missed its import. Self-denial is a prerequisite to discipleship, he says. "One cannot follow me unless he denies himself." These are not enticing words. There is no design about them to attract the masses. Jesus does not offer material goods; he demands material goods of his followers, and he expects them to meet his demands.

"You must take up your cross," he continues.

Christian discipleship will be a heavy burden. A wooden cross is not easy to lift; it is difficult to carry. His audience knew that bearing a cross involved more than carrying a burden. They knew that the cross was the severest type of punishment Rome inflicted on a criminal. The culprit convicted of a capital crime had to carry his cross, his instrument of death, to the place of his execution. He was thereby expected to participate actively in his own death. The Jews were careful in every way not to offend the Romans. Theirs was a slave society. The slave had to obey his master. He had to use every means at his disposal to please him. Condemnation as a criminal and death on the cross was to the Jew the most hideous of all prospects. He spent his whole life trying to avoid the hammer blow of his Roman master. Rome had dispossessed the Jew of his independence. He had nothing left but his life; he intended to keep it at any cost.

But Jesus said to them that if life itself is the most important thing they have, so that they must preserve it by whatever means, they really do not have anything at all. In the end, they will lose that. It is counterproductive to live just to live. It is like Hilary, in the West End London play, *The Old Country*. His wife says of him that all he has is "Hilary thinking about Hilary thinking about Hilary." Life, just for the sake of life, is empty. It is utterly futile.

When people have something more important than life itself to challenge them, something worth working for and even worth dying for, they can be said to live. The gospel is of so great importance that when people lose their lives for it they really find life. The good news of the message of Jesus is life everlasting.

No treasure is equal to the value of a person's soul. There is nothing so precious that we would exchange our soul for it. *Soul* can best be understood in modern terms as personality. Who would give up his personality, his self-hood, for anything else in all the world? But self-hood finds fulfillment only in Jesus. If we are ashamed of him, we cannot find self-fulfillment. Unless we are willing to declare ourselves openly for him and his gospel, he will not declare himself for us in the presence of God. If we are not openly on the side of Christ in this world, we cannot expect anything from him in the world to come.

This brings us to one of the most difficult verses in the Bible to understand. Jesus says that there are some standing in the crowd listening to him who will not die until they have seen the Kingdom of God come with power. Most people think that this means they will not die until the end of the world, when this temporal order is displaced by God's eternal order. They think that Jesus expected the end of the world was coming soon and that his death and resurrection would usher it in. Thus they think that Jesus was mistaken. But Jesus was not in error. What the passage means is that there are some in that crowd who will not die until long after Pentecost. They themselves will receive the power of the Holy Spirit.

The coming of the Kingdom of God in power, in this instance, is the establishment of the Christian church.

## THE TRANSFIGURATION AND ITS AFTERMATH
### (9:2-29)

Peter's confession that Jesus is the Messiah was confirmed by a disclosure from God on the Mount of Transfiguration. Mark does not attempt to identify the place, other than to explain that it is a high mountain—the New Testament equivalent of the Old Testament Mount Sinai. Generally, unless it is a private vision of an individual, divine disclosure takes place on a mountaintop. The supreme instance of it in the Old Testament was God's giving the Ten Commandments to Moses. In the New Testament, the Transfiguration is the supreme instance of divine disclosure.

Jesus took only Peter, James, and John with him for this experience. He did not take the other nine disciples, because he had less confidence in them. Some persons clamor for a classless society; but classes, or hierarchies, develop in human society by nature. Equal opportunity does not assure equal achievement. The church began with its hierarchy. There were degrees of difference even among the apostles. There has never been a classless society, and there never will be. Capitulation to mediocrity is the greatest of all social dangers. There must be leadership based on exceptional performance. Peter, James, and John were more perceptive because they

65

were more receptive to Jesus than the rest. He chose them to go with him because they were the only ones equal to what was about to take place on that mountain top.

They marveled at what they saw. Jesus was transformed before their very eyes. His clothes became bright like light and so white that there was no earthly whiteness its equal. This was a preview of what he would look like after his resurrection. In personal features and garments, he shone like the sun.

Then Elijah and Moses appeared and engaged in conversation with Jesus. Why does Mark place Elijah's name first, before Moses'? Both chronologically and in importance as an historical figure, Moses takes precedence over Elijah, for Moses is the greatest figure in Jewish history. There may be no reason why Mark lists them as he does. Elijah no doubt represents prophecy, while Moses is the personification of the Law. Both are heralds of the Messiah, but each in turn will be superseded by the Messiah.

Peter proposes to build three tabernacles, one for each of them—Elijah, Moses, and Jesus. Then a cloud descends and they hear the voice of God. To his people in the exodus from Egypt, God had appeared in the cloud by day and the pillar of fire by night. In the Old Testament, the voice of God often comes forth out of a cloud, the *Shekinah*. The voice says, "This is my beloved Son: hear him" (Mark 9:7b). The vision is over; they look around, and all they see is Jesus. The Messiah needs no visible support. He is, in himself, the all-sufficient agent of God.

As they walk down the slope of the mountain, the disciples recall that the scribes teach that Elijah must first come. Jesus confirms this, and he reminds them that Elijah has already come. They themselves saw him on the mountain. And John the Baptist—though Jesus does not call his name—fulfilled Elijah's role as the forerunner, and they know what happened to him.

When they rejoined the other nine, they found them in the midst of a crowd, where some scribes were questioning them. There was great confusion, and everyone ran up to Jesus as soon as he came into view. When Jesus inquired what was the matter, a man stepped up and said, "I brought my son to your disciples that they might exorcise him of a demon, but they could not." The son was evidently an epileptic, and he suffered one of his fits in Jesus' presence. Before Jesus exorcised the evil spirit and healed the boy, he asked the father if he could believe, for he assured him that anything is possible to anyone who believes. The father replied, "Lord, I can try to believe, and where I fail, I ask you to help me." That was enough. Jesus cast the demon out and ordered him never to come back again. The son looked lifeless, his last seizure had been so devastating. Yet, Jesus took him by the hand and he got up.

There are two remarkable features to this story. First, one does not have to believe fully—he needs only to want sincerely to believe—in order for the Lord to help him. Second, the confidence and trust of the father in the power of Jesus was sufficient to cure the son. Intercession is a powerful ingredient of the Christian faith. Jesus told his disciples that they had failed to help the boy because they had not prayed enough. The use of the power of God, he said, comes only as a result of fasting and prayer.

In his magnificent painting of the Transfiguration, Raphael includes the healing of the boy. The Transfiguration does not stand apart from this miracle: it incorporates it. Without it, the Transfiguration itself would be incomplete. The Messiah is a serving Messiah.

Mark employs the incident of the Transfiguration as a peg on which to hang a bundle of teachings. As we have seen already, the Evangelist is given to aphorisms. A truth is annunciated. It is not amplified or explained.

After the healing of the epileptic boy, Jesus makes his second prediction of his passion and death, just as he had made the first prediction after Peter's confession at Caesarea Philippi. The disciples did not understand what he meant when he made this prediction. They were hesitant to ask him, for they realized that they should have known and that the Master would be disappointed by their ignorance. Instead, Jesus asked them what they talked about on the way. They did not answer his question, because they were embarrassed to admit to him that each one of them wanted to be esteemed by Jesus as the greatest of the lot and to rank first with him. He knew what they had been thinking, without their telling him; so he took a little child in his arms, and said,

"Whoever receives one of the children receives me." Greatness in life does not come from what people do for us, or from the exalted position we may hold in their eyes. Greatness comes from what we do for others, and from the privileges and advantages we give up in their behalf. Therefore, he who desired to be first in Jesus' eyes must be last in the eyes of secular-minded people.

John called the Master's attention to a person who, though outside the circle of his followers, was nonetheless casting out devils in Jesus' name. Jesus told John not to interfere with the man's work, for he said that he who is not against us is for us. Judge a person not by what he professes, but by what he does. The quality of one's works is of more significance than the nature of his opinions. Even a cup of water given in Christ's name will be rewarded; whereas any offense to a young, struggling believer, especially a little child, will be severely punished. It would be better for one to have a heavy millstone hung from his neck and to be drowned, than to cause offense to any of Christ's little ones.

Therefore, the hand, the foot, and even the eye are of less importance to us than a pure heart and a righteous character. If one of these organs should cause us to fall into temptation and to offend God, that organ should be severed from our body. It is more profitable to go through life maimed than to be cast into hell. Salt is a preservative, but it is useless when it loses its strength. We need to be concerned that we are preserved through righteousness and are able thereby to live at peace with one another.

## DISCIPLESHIP
(10:1-31)

From a secular point of view, discipleship is not an advantage but a liability. One pays a price for it, and its rewards are generally deferred. Divorce, for example, which was permitted among the Jews, was disavowed by Jesus. He did not countenance divorce for his followers. Consequently, when the Pharisees said that Moses permitted bills of divorcement, by which marriages were legally set aside, Jesus responded that Moses did this as a concession to human wickedness. His act was not an expression of the will of God. God's intention in marriage was established in the creation, when he made woman as the correlate to man. Neither could find fulfillment without the other. In their marital union they became one flesh. "What therefore God hath joined together, let no man put asunder" (Mark 10:9). Jesus explained to his disciples that whenever a divorced person marries, the divorcee commits adultery in his or her sexual relationships with the newly acquired spouse.

In the male-dominated society of Judaism, adultery was defined as sexual relations between a married woman and some man other than her husband. She was said by her illicit act to commit adultery against her husband. If a married man

70

engaged in sexual relationships with a woman other than his wife, he did not commit adultery against his wife. He did, however, commit adultery against the woman's husband. If the woman was not married, he did not commit adultery against anyone, only fornication. But Jesus puts women on the same level as men. He says that a man can commit adultery against his wife and that a woman can commit adultery against her husband. This is a new moral precept and a strict adherence to the inviolate nature of the marriage vow.

People began then to bring their children to Jesus, whereas, before, if children had accompanied their parents, they were kept in the background and not allowed to say anything or to intrude upon the scene of the Master's work. When, in another instance, Jesus sought out a child in the crowd, he selected a child merely as an example of what he was talking about at the time; here, however, the situation is different. The parents are taking the initiative: they want their children to see Jesus. They are eager for Jesus to bless their little ones.

The disciples are annoyed, thinking that Jesus does not have time for such interruptions. Every moment is precious, and the Master must use this time for those who understand. His efforts will be wasted on irresponsible children.

But Jesus does not view the children as irresponsible. He orders the disciples to let them through. He takes the children in his arms and blesses them. In fact, he tells the disciples that unless they become as responsive and receptive as little children, they cannot enter the Kingdom of God. The emphasis here is not on the innocence of children—that they are too young to be contaminated by sin—but on their natural receptivity. Children are eager to receive any kindness anyone wants to bestow on them. They are helpless, and they place utter dependence upon others to care for them. This is the way disciples of Christ must be. They cannot do anything for themselves. They must receive grace with open hands. They must realize that they are absolutely dependent on God.

The encounter with the rich man follows naturally upon this incident where Jesus receives the children. Riches will not buy one's salvation. In fact, riches are more likely to be an encumbrance than an asset. Mark tells us that a man who came running to Jesus fell down on his knees and asked Jesus what he must do to inherit eternal life. He saluted Jesus with the title, "Good Master."

Our Lord's response was unusual. He said, "Why do you call me good? There is none good but God!" Does this mean that Jesus recognized himself as a sinner, as being no different from the man who asked him the question? Not at all! We must seek to reconstruct the situation. The man is excited. He falls on his knees in the form and, perhaps, in the pretense of worship. In saluting Jesus he said more than the situation warranted, since he had never seen Jesus before. As a devout Jew, he had learned that worship belonged only to God. In Jewish teaching, no one was completely good—that is, righteous and holy—but God himself. Jesus meant by his reply, only, "You don't know me. You do not realize who I am. What right have you to flatter me with such praise? You know full well that what you ascribe to me belongs only to God."

That the man was a devout Jew is evidenced by what he says. He kept the Ten Commandments; perhaps that was enough for a Jew. Yet many others had not kept the commandments. But his keeping the Ten Commandments was not a sufficient achievement for him to become a disciple of Jesus. Jesus told him that there was more required of him: he would have to dispose of his wealth—all of it. Only then would he be free to become one of his disciples. The man turned away when he heard that condition. He could not do what Jesus asked. He had too much wealth; he loved too much what he had. His dependence upon material things turned him away from the Kingdom of God. Discipleship was too costly for him.

People of the Orient often use exaggerated language to make a point. They speak in hyperboles. Jesus was no exception. He told the disciples that it is as hard for a rich man to get to heaven as it is for a camel to go through the eye of a needle. The disciples were shocked by what he said. "Nobody will get there, then," they retorted, for they expected to be rewarded for following him. But Jesus enlarged their understanding by adding, "All things are possible with God." The man who turned away should have realized that his riches could not help him. Nothing one does can win God's favor. All of us alike, rich and poor, are absolutely dependent on God. It is his unmerited kindness, his undeserved mercy, his free grace, which saves us all. If riches are a hindrance to our salvation, it is because we ourselves have made them so. We have let them and what they can buy be more attractive to us than God and the demands of his kingdom. Rather than give up our wealth, by surrendering it all to God and the needs of God's people, we walk away from the obligations of discipleship.

It is most interesting that Jesus' observations on the perils of riches are followed—nay, interrupted—by Peter's almost desperate question: "If what you say is true, then what can we, your followers, expect? We have given up everything we own for you. Don't we, by making this sacrifice and by becoming your disciples, have the right to expect something for ourselves?" Our Lord's answer is very significant:

There is no man that hath left house, or brethren, or sisters, or father, or mother, or wife, or children, or lands, for my sake and the gospel's, But he shall receive a hundredfold now in this time, houses, and brethren, and sisters, and mothers, and children, and lands, with persecutions; and in the world to come eternal life (Mark 10:29b-30).

In other words, deprivations because of Christ are more than compensated for, even in this life, by the benefits and rewards of discipleship. Our Lord does not state this in terms of an exchange of material goods for spiritual gifts, as we might expect; rather, he states it in terms of a multiplication of the very same things that we are asked to give up, for those things are given back to us in superabundance by

God. In the list, the only item surrendered that is not returned is "wife." For one thing, in the light of his Jewish conviction on monogamy, he could not sanction the multiplication of spouses. And, likewise, in keeping with his earlier teaching against divorce, he could not promise the gift of a new wife for the loss by divorce of an old one. Family ties that are broken will be restored, however, in a richer and fuller way, through Christian fellowship, in which all relationships will be strengthened and enriched. Material wealth is not to be excluded. What accrues through mutual support and sharing will be greater in the long run than anything that one person can ever hope selfishly to accumulate for himself. Do not expect all this to happen without resistance and persecution, and never for one moment forget that those persons who are first in the secular order are bound to be last in the spiritual order, where only goodness counts.

## GREATNESS
(10:32-52)

At this juncture, and for the first time, Saint Mark mentions Jerusalem in connection with the itinerary of Jesus. Most of our Lord's ministry had taken place in Galilee. The messianic disclosures have happened in the gentile territory north and east of Galilee, and in the environs of Capernaum, as Jesus and his disciples passed back through Galilee on their way south. Now Saint Mark says explicitly that they were

75

on the way going up to Jerusalem. He states that Jesus went before them and that "they were amazed; and, as they followed, they were afraid." The crowd itself was apprehensive about the trip to Jerusalem. Instinctively, they began to feel that things might not go as well there as they had gone in Galilee. But it was only with the twelve disciples that Jesus shared his inmost thoughts. To them he made his third prediction of the Passion.

His first prediction of the Passion came in connection with Peter's confession of Jesus' messiahship, and the second in connection with the Transfiguration. The third prediction is not made in relation to any special event. It is made merely as he and the disciples are walking along the wayside, now separated from the crowd, drawing closer to Jerusalem. When he had finished his second discourse on discipleship, and just before two incidents—one an encounter with two of his disciples, and the other a miracle at Jericho—Jesus interspersed his third prediction of his own passion. But it is somewhat different from the other two predictions. It is far more explicit in its details, so much so that most commentators think that Mark amplified Jesus' remarks and attributed to him what Mark himself clearly knew had actually happened. I do not agree. Jesus realized what was about to happen to him before it occurred. He knew his enemies and their method of operation. He foresaw that the chief priests and the scribes would condemn him to death. It would be the gentiles who would carry out their work for them, since the only authority which could execute the death penalty was Roman authority. It was inevitable that they would mock him and scourge him and spit on him; yet, through it all, his followers should not forget that on the third day he would rise from the dead.

This third prediction has no follow-up. In fact, it is rudely interrupted by James and John, who ask Jesus to give them what they are about to ask him. They want to be seated at his right and at his left when he comes into his kingdom.

They had not apprehended anything at all about his passion, because they were preoccupied in thinking only of their own advancement. That frequently happens to all of us. We do not hear the needs of another as he tells us about those needs, simply because we are thinking all the while only about our own wishes and how they can be fulfilled. Jesus sadly responds by asking them if they are able to endure what he will be called upon to endure; that is, do they really understand the obligations and hardships that must go along with such recognition? They assure him of their hardihood and competence to take on anything that he can in the cause. Jesus does not argue with them; he accepts their boast as if it were no boast. All he says is, "What you request is not within my power to grant. That, after all, is left entirely to God." When the other ten disciples heard this request, they were indignant at James and John. Not only was their presumption unbearable, but, in their effort to promote themselves, they had overlooked and disregarded the interests of all the rest. In this, their action was insufferable.

Jesus seems to have ignored it all. He does not take up the argument for the other ten. After all, he knew that any one of them would have requested the same thing for himself, also, if he had had the chance.

Rather, he uses this incident to tell them what true greatness really is. It is not what the Roman world has defined it to be. It does not come through earthly power, through authority and might that overpowers other people. Rome made her conquests by the sword. Her great ones are they who have power and exercise authority. True greatness, Jesus says, is service, and the greatest person is he who would be the servant of all. The more one serves, the greater he becomes.

Jesus then reverts to his prediction of his passion. He says that he came only to save and to give his life as ransom for many. Here the nature of messiahship is clearly defined. The Messiah of God is the messianic Servant.

It was at Jericho that the blind beggar Bartimaeus sat by the highway along which Jesus and his followers journeyed. When he perceived the approaching crowd and heard from the people that it was Jesus, he began to cry out to him. The people rebuked him. After all, he was just one among many. Jesus had no time to stop and give him personal attention. But the beggar knew that this was his only chance; so, rather than being quiet, he began to cry louder. He was determined to be heard and helped. And Jesus heard him. He told the people to send the man to him. He commended Bartimaeus for his great faith, and he cured him.

This is the very last miracle Jesus performed before he entered Jerusalem. He gave sight to this blind beggar, and the beggar joined the disciples and followed Jesus.

But there is something more to the story than the cure. It is what the blind man called Jesus. He cried out, "Jesus, thou Son of David, have mercy on me." "Son of David" was the title of the Messiah. Jesus did not tell him to be quiet, as he had commanded the devils who had recognized him. Rather, he accepted the tribute.

The messiahship, which at first had been apprehended only by the devils, and gradually by the disciples, was now known by everybody. It had been disclosed through Jesus' acts of service. Now everybody knew that the true Messiah had come—and he wore the garb of a servant.

CHAPTER THREE
PERSONAL REFLECTION

1. What significance does the relationship between Peter and Jesus hold for the other disciples? What can it mean for us in our own day?

2. Why are self-denial and self-sacrifice necessary actions for the Christian? List some ways you might practice self-denial and self-sacrifice.

3. What is the basis upon which one receives salvation? How does Jesus tell his disciples about this?

4. Reflect upon what Jesus meant when he said "All things are possible with God" (10:27).

5. How do you understand the concept of greatness as revealed in the messiahship of Jesus? What does this mean for your personal life?

80

### CHAPTER FOUR

# THE PROPHETIC SERVANT
## (Mark 11–13)

### THE TRIUMPHAL ENTRY
#### (11:1-11)

*S*aint Mark compresses Jesus' entire ministry in Jerusalem into one short week. Yet we are indebted to this evangelist for Holy Week, for it is he who indicates the days of the week and tells us what happened on each particular day. Bethany, Jesus' haven of refuge and place of quiet retreat, is the dividing line between each of the successive days. After his witness during the waking hours, he returns to Bethany to spend the night. It is just a short way over the Mount of Olives from the Holy City; so a good brisk walk to and from Jerusalem began and ended every day for Jesus.

Some scholars feel that the celebration of Holy Week had already become a tradition in the early church when Mark began to compose his Gospel. They detect an artificiality in his treatment of the Jerusalem mission, as if he felt obligated to make everything fit into the six-day span between the two Sabbaths. It is their opinion that Mark crowds into Holy Week what really does not belong there, that he transposes into this last week certain events from

Jesus' earlier visits to Jerusalem. It could be, of course, the other way. It could be that Mark's careful delineation of the days and events of Holy Week was the catalyst for the church to bring it to the special commemorative place it now holds in Christendom. Be that as it may, Mark does attach pedagogical significance to all that happened while Jesus was in Jerusalem. Since there is a special lesson connected with everything that Jesus did and said, this whole time may be thought of as a period of instruction. Mark operated from a definite theological perspective, portraying Jesus as the dedicated servant of God. Jesus was obedient to God, and rendered through his service inestimable good to humankind.

Jesus displayed through his work in Galilee that he was the servant of his people and the servant of the Lord. In the gentile territory beyond Galilee, as he journeyed toward Jerusalem, he revealed himself to be the true messianic servant. So now his mission in Jerusalem becomes that of the prophet. We see him now as the prophetic servant, showing his people the things of God.

To understand his work in Jerusalem, we need to know what it means to be called a prophet. In the Old Testament, a prophet is primarily a spokesman of God. What he says is not his own, but what God gives him to say. He does not know how to speak for himself. He is always and invariably the voice of someone else. "Then the Lord put forth his hand and touched my mouth" (Jeremiah 1:9). The message of the prophet is God's message, and the prophet himself is God's champion. In any controversy between God and his people, the prophet is never on the side of the people: he is always on God's side. He does not know how to be the attorney for the defense. He is the prosecuting attorney of the Lord.

Hear the word of the Lord, ye children of Israel: for the Lord hath a controversy with the inhabitants of the land, Because *there is* no truth, nor mercy, nor knowledge of God in the land (Hosea 4:1).

Sometimes, of course, the prophet foretells the future, predicting events.

And it shall come to pass in the last days, *that* the mountain of the Lord's house shall be established in the top of the mountains, and shall be exalted above the hills; and all the nations shall flow unto it. And many people shall go and say, Come ye, and let us go up to the mountain of the Lord, to the house of the God of Jacob; and he will teach us his ways, and we will walk in his paths: for out of Zion shall go forth the law, and the word of the Lord from Jerusalem. And he shall judge among the nations, and shall rebuke many people: and they shall beat their swords into plowshares, and their spears into pruning hooks: nation shall not lift up sword against nation, neither shall they learn war any more (Isaiah 2:2-4).

We shall see in these three chapters how Jesus fills these several roles of the prophet. Though he remains the servant, he is the prophetic servant, dominated and controlled by the eternal word of God.

This disclosure of Jesus in the role of the prophet begins on Palm Sunday, when Jesus made his grand entry into Jerusalem. Not only does Palm Sunday begin Holy Week, it also serves as the transition in

Mark's account from the messianic servant to the prophetic servant. Indeed, the entrance of Jesus into Jerusalem is a messianic entrance. Jesus fulfills what is expected of the Messiah, and he pictures the true nature of the Messiah and his work. He rides into the city in triumph, accepting the homage of the people in the same way that kings accept the homage of their subjects. But Jesus does not ride in on an Arabian steed, a magnificent charger, but on a beast of burden, a lowly ass. He is the conquering Messiah, but he conquers by humble service.

Why did Jesus ride at all? It was not his custom. The way he had always travelled, and for great distances at that, had been on foot. He would return to Bethany on foot, and on each of the succeeding days he would return to Jerusalem on foot. But not on this day! Jesus rode because the Messiah was expected to ride. If he did not ride, it would appear that he had repudiated his messiahship. What he had once permitted to be whispered only in secret, he now declared aloud as if from the housetops. Blind Bartimaeus had heralded the event. This poor beggar had been the Elijah and the John the Baptist of the triumphal entry into Jerusalem.

Zechariah had accurately foretold both of the motives governing Jesus' entrance into Jerusalem, when he prophesied the coming of the Messiah:

Rejoice greatly, O daughter of Zion; shout, O daughter of Jerusalem: behold, thy King cometh unto thee: he *is* just, and having salvation; lowly, and riding upon an ass, and upon a colt the foal of an ass (Zechariah 9:9).

Jesus sent two of the disciples ahead of him and the crowd. They were told where to find the ass. He would be standing tied outside a house at the crossroads of a village. The disciples were to unloose him and bring him to Jesus. If anyone should try to stop the disciples or inquire what right they had to the colt, all they had to do was to tell the persons that the Lord had need of the animal, and they would let them have it.

Was the owner of the ass one of Jesus' followers? If so, all the disciples had to do was to identify themselves as Jesus' emissaries. Whatever Jesus might want, his followers were happy to supply. Who would not welcome the opportunity to accommodate God's Messiah?

There is significance in the fact that the little animal had never been used before. Jesus' ride that day would break him in. Antiquity laid great stress on the requirement that kings, potentates, the great of the land, make their grand entrances on untrained, unused, beasts of burden. They could not accept anything secondhand. This would be the people's expectation of their Messiah.

The crowds threw their outer garments in the way before him, thereby making a covering for the road on which he journeyed. Others cut fronds from the trees and cast them before him. All cried, "Hosannah!" which is a cry for help or deliverance. It can be addressed either to God or to an earthly king. In this instance it means quite literally, "Save us! Save us now! God save us!"

This cry fits perfectly the messianic expectation.

The Messiah would come for no other purpose than to save God's people. Indeed, he would be God's instrument in their deliverance. He would put all their enemies under their feet.

And this is the impression Jesus intended to convey. He had come as their Savior. But the way in which he would save them was not the way they anticipated. The triumphal entry is the climax of the messianic disclosure. It is succeeded by the prophetic disclosure which gives content and relief to the messianic concept.

## JUDGMENT
### (11:12-26)

The first act of Jesus in his role as the prophetic servant was to instruct the people in the harsh lesson of the judgment of the Lord. It is not enough to think of "the gentle Jesus, meek and mild." We must think of him, also, as standing with a whip in his hand in the Temple, and castigating an unfruitful tree on the roadside.

The second day of Holy Week is directed to the lesson of divine wrath and judgment. Only two incidents, according to Saint Mark, take place on that day. Both are made of the same piece, and each strengthens and confirms the other. In fact, here again is Mark's typical way of doing things. Here is another example of his unique style of writing. As he did earlier, with Jairus's sick, dying daughter and with the Syrophoenician woman, Mark interrupts one incident in order to present another. He begins with Jesus and the fig tree. He moves on to the scene in the Temple. Then, he goes back to tell us what happened to the fig tree.

It seems that on his second day Jesus had left Bethany without breakfast. He was very hungry. He saw a fig tree, green with leaves, on the way ahead. The appearance of the tree led him to think that it had an abundance of fruit on it, though he knew that it was not the season for figs. He ran up to it. When he got there, he was disappointed because there was no fruit. He then addressed the tree and told it that henceforth it would never bear fruit again. It was worthless because it had not satisfied his hunger. The next day, when he and his disciples passed by, they saw that the fig tree was dead.

This seems unfair. If it was not the season for figs, why should Jesus treat the little tree in such an outrageous manner? However, when we use the word *unfair* or *unjust,* we presuppose a human element. We treat the tree as if it had personality, as if it were a real, discriminating, feeling person like ourselves. It is not possible to be unfair or unjust to an inanimate object. The little tree belonged to Jesus, the Lord of creation. He who made it could do with it as he pleased. In destroying the tree he provided an object lesson to his followers. What the disciples saw, they would never forget. If Jesus would do that to a tree simply because it did not yield fruit when it was not the season for fruit, think what God will do to us when we do not produce—since we are able and expected to do so. We, too, will wither and die, just as the little tree did.

Then our divine Lord deduces a second lesson from the withered fig tree. He uses it as an example of power. Peter said, "behold, the fig tree which thou cursedst is withered away" (Mark 11:21b). And Jesus answered,

Whosoever shall say unto this mountain, Be thou removed, and be thou cast into the sea; and shall not doubt in his heart, but shall believe that those things which he saith shall come to pass; he shall have whatsoever he saith (Mark 11:23b).

If we really believe when we pray, what we pray for will come about. But Jesus cautions his disciples, "When ye stand praying, forgive, . . . if ye do not forgive, neither will your Father which is in heaven forgive your trespasses" (Mark 11:25-26).

Even in the demonstration of power, there is that spiritual element which must be taken into account. Jesus seems not to have done this in the way he behaved with the fig tree. It appears that he gave way to anger, that he was unreasonable in his expectations and acted unseemly when he destroyed the tree. Not so! In teaching a lesson, the teacher often must assume the pose of the pupil. We might have been angry on such an occasion; he was not. He simply asked the disciples to realize that it is dangerous for any created thing ever to displease its creator. God is just as much a God of wrath and judgment, and capable of inflicting punishment, as he is a God of mercy and love, and capable of granting forgiveness.

88

Jesus showed the wrath of God when he took a whip in his hands and lashed the produce merchants and the money changers and drove them out of the court of the Temple. It was not appropriate for them to be in a place of worship. I often think of this scene when I visit a postcard stand and vendor's stall with colored dishes, picture books, and other souvenirs in the narthex of a cathedral. The merchants and money changers operated in the Court of the Gentiles, the one place in the Temple area where anybody, no matter who he was, could come. What strangers saw in the Court of the Gentiles influenced their attitude toward God and the worship of God. Jesus said, as he drove these merchants out, "Is it not written, My house shall be called of all nations the house of prayer? but ye have made it a den of thieves" (Mark 11:17b).

## CONTROVERSY WITH THE JEWISH LEADERS
(11:27–12:27)

Jesus' third day in Jerusalem is crowded with activity, most of it taking place in and about the Temple. Saint Mark tells us that after the walk from Bethany back to Jerusalem in the very early morning, our Lord went with them immediately to the Temple. What he taught on this third day was largely the result of his various encounters with the Jewish leadership. His teachings are in the form of answers he gave to their various questions. His teaching on this day issues from controversy, from a series of hostile confrontations.

The first controversy was with the chief priests, the scribes, and the elders—an impressive group of people. In them were embodied the characteristics which the Jews cherished most: ceremonial worship (the priests), knowledge of the law (the scribes), and wisdom based on long experience (the elders). These people belonged to the Sanhedrin, the supreme religious council of the Jewish people and the highest governing body of the country other than the Romans. It was the custom in that day for teachers to walk about in the colonnade of the Court of the Gentiles, talking to their disciples, lecturing directly to them and also fielding their questions. Jesus did the same.

It was in this situation that the confrontation took place. Jewish religious authorities and critics of Jesus infiltrated the ranks of his followers. They were indignant that on the previous day he had taken it on himself to overturn the tables of the money changers and drive out the merchants from their stalls. The merchants and the money changers had paid for their concessions to do business in the Court of the Gentiles. The Temple profited financially from their trade. This new teacher abandoned all the techniques of the teaching profession. He did not raise questions and suggest possible answers for the public to consider. He did not pose problems and modestly offer tentative solutions. His answers were definitive, and he voiced final and absolute solutions. He spoke and acted in an arbitrary and dictatorial manner.

So these religious leaders said to Jesus, "By what authority do you say what you say and do what you do?"

Authority is basic in religion. Systematic theology begins with the doctrine of authority. We must make clear what our basic presuppositions are. Out of what do we derive those beliefs we cherish and by which we live? From the Bible? From the church? From an "infallible" teacher like the Pope? From the trial and error of experience? From the application of reason? Or from a combination of many things?

Unfortunately for us, Jesus does not answer this question posed by the Jewish leaders. He knows they are not sincere. They are just out to trick him. Consequently, at this juncture, posterity is denied the benefit of an irrefutable answer from him who is the source of all truth.

Jesus counters their question with one of his own. He realized that the best defense is offense. He did not try to repulse his enemies; instead, he attacked them. "I will make a bargain with you," he replied. "You tell me whether John the Baptist spoke for God or for men. Was his message divinely inspired or only humanly motivated?" He had them. If they said that John had spoken for God, he could reply, "Why didn't you believe him then?" If they said that John's opinions were his own, their own authority would be jeopardized—they would lose the people, because the people thought John the Baptist was a prophet.

Therefore, Jesus did not get any answer from

them, and they did not get one from him. He had beaten the Jewish leadership at its own game. In worldly cunning he had outwitted the wittiest of them who, constantly practicing worldly cunning, generally outwitted everyone else.

It is in this vein that Jesus tells the story of the rich landowner who rented his farms to tenants and went away into another land. Most of the property was in vineyards. The rent the tenants were expected to pay was in produce. They gave the owner the major portion of what they raised. They and their families lived off the land and were permitted to keep a share of the grapes to sell for their own profit. The greater the yield, the greater the prosperity, both for the owner and for themselves. But these tenants were greedy. They dealt bodily harm to the servants whom the landlord sent to them. Later, when the landlord persisted in trying to collect his rent, they killed those he sent to them. When he commissioned his own son to go out and require the tenants to honor their contract, they killed the son, also. They reasoned that if the landlord had no heir the property would fall to them because they were on it and had worked it so long as if it were their own.

It was not unusual in Jesus' day for a foreigner of wealth to buy property in a province such a Judea and go back to his home in Antioch or Athens or some other city and expect rent from the Jewish tenants whom he had placed on the land. Likewise, if the owner died without heirs, the persons who tended the property could claim it as their own. But if the owner himself came and exercised the prerogatives that were his under Roman law, then those murderous tenants could be put to death.

We have seen that Mark does not record many of the parables of Jesus. This story is not a parable: it is, like that of the sower and the soil, an allegory. Every part of the story has a special meaning. The vineyard is Israel, the owner is God, the wicked tenants are the Jewish people. The servants the Jews mistreat and finally kill are the prophets, and the son is Jesus of Nazareth himself.

The Jewish leaders immediately got the point of the story. They recognized that he spoke of themselves. They were indignant and wanted to arrest him, but they were afraid to assail him further in the midst of his followers. They could only walk away.

But they did not give up. Soon they were at him again. This time, however, they employed surrogates: the Pharisees, who were teachers but not necessarily from the ruling class; and the Herodians, who championed the Jewish Herod over the Roman Pilate. Since A.D. 6 the Jews had had to pay a head tax in addition to a property tax. The head tax required each person to contribute something to the state, to the Roman overlord. The Jews hated this tax. When it was first enacted, riots broke out in Jerusalem and in other cities throughout the region.

The Pharisees and the Herodians devised a subtle trap for Jesus. They began by complimenting him: "We know how wise you are. Tell us, should we pay taxes to Caesar?" The tax had to be paid in Roman coinage. If Jesus supported the tax, he would lose the people, for all of them were against it. If he disavowed the tax, he would offend Rome and would be liable to punishment as a traitor.

People in ancient times thought of coinage as belonging to the ruler who had it minted and whose image was always stamped on it. It was thought to be his personal property.

Jesus asked to be shown a coin. By asking whose image was on the coin, he reminded the people about this popular concept of imperial ownership. When he got the answer, "Caesar's," he said simply, "Well, give him but what is his anyway. Render to him what he owns." The clincher is what follows: "But give to God what belongs to him, too. Render to him what is rightfully his."

The most violent Jewish opponents of Rome could not object to that answer. They knew that God is the creator and possessor of everybody and everything, and even Caesar himself belonged to God. The sagacity of Solomon was present in Jesus of Nazareth. Here was Solomonic wisdom at its best. The interlocutors had no reply. They stood in amazement at what Jesus had said.

The last encounter was with the Sadducees. They confronted Jesus with the issue of life after death. Though they did not believe in immortality, they knew that he did. They rejected the concept of resurrection, and Jesus taught the resurrection of the dead.

The Sadducees reminded Jesus of Moses' instruction, that if a man died childless, his next younger brother—the brother, therefore, next to him in primogeniture—should marry his wife and rear his brother's children as if they were his own. The Sadducees asked Jesus what would become of a wife in heaven if she had been required to marry seven brothers in one family. Which one of them would be her husband after the resurrection, and to which man would she be wife?

Jesus answered that in heaven such relationships as marriage and the acquiring and disposing of property do not exist. Heaven is not comparable to anything we know on earth. Here, we are limited by our humanity. There, we are totally free, because we share God's divinity.

Jesus was eager to disavow any messianic concept that was based on Jewish nationalism and patriotism. People in heaven will not be like Jews here on earth. They will be like the angels of God.

The Sadducees based their religious and theological ideas on the Pentateuch—that is, the first five books of the Old Testament, which they believed had been written by Moses, the greatest teacher and lawgiver their nation had produced. They found nothing in those books that promised individual life after death or that assured anybody of his own resurrection. Jesus said that the Sadducees were mistaken in their interpretation of the Pentateuch, that they did not see the true implications in the teaching of Moses. For example, when God spoke to Moses out of the burning bush on Mount Horeb, he used the present tense. He did not say, *"I was* the God of Abraham, Isaac, and Jacob." He said, *"I am* the God of Abraham, Isaac, and Jacob."

The Sadducees in their interpretation had limited the present tense to God himself as the subject of the sentence. They knew that he was alive. They thought that sentence meant only that it was God whom Abraham, Isaac, and Jacob worshipped and served while they lived on earth, and that, now, that same God offers himself to Moses. Moses is to be their successor; but Jesus tells the Sadducees they stopped too soon. If God is defined as being the God of Abraham, Isaac, and Jacob, then they are necessary to his identification. Therefore, if he is living, they, too, are living, and they are living with him.

Jesus is using here the same rabbinic subtlety that other Jewish teachers used. He is employing the weapons of his enemies. What this means to us is simply that if God thought enough of people to create them in his own image and to love them and to have fellowship with them here on earth, he will certainly not throw them away. He will keep that relationship with them forever; death cannot sever it. God will raise them up from the dead and give them an exalted place in his presence in heaven.

## INSTRUCTION AND INSPIRATION
### (12:28-44)

Chapter twelve appropriately closes on four incidents, all of which provide important instruction, and three of which give us some inspiration as well.

One of the scribes, listening to Jesus in his disputations and observing the way in which he handled himself under confrontation and in controversy, was favorably impressed, and he addressed a positive question to Jesus: "Which," he said, "is the first commandment?" He meant by this, "What, precisely, is the essence of the Law? What is at the top of the hierarchy of all commandments?"

Jesus' answer may not have seemed altogether new to the Jews of his day. A quarter of a century before the birth of Jesus, Hillel, the great rabbi, had written: "What you yourself hate, do not do to your fellow; this is the whole law; the rest is commentary; go and learn it." The most prevalent attitude, however, was to keep all the laws punctiliously. Hence innumerable commentaries on the same, with their instructions on how to do it!

Jesus said that the essence of the Law is simply to love God completely, with mind, heart, soul, and strength, and to love one's neighbor as oneself. There has been much debate over what "neighbor" really meant to Jesus and his contemporaries. Even in the severity of that day the Jews included the foreigners who dwelt beside them in their own country. What more is needed than that? *Neighbor* is anyone with whom we have contacts and relationships. In Jesus' day, the neighborhood was small; now, instant communication has made the whole world one neighborhood. The application is the same. We are to love and hold in a loving relationship anyone with whom we have contact. We love the neighbor because we love God and because God loves our neighbor. If we do not love the neighbor, we then impair our love for God.

The scribe complimented Jesus on his answer. After that, Saint Mark tells us, nobody else asked him any more questions.

Instead, Jesus addressed to his audience a purely rhetorical question. Though Jesus does not answer it, the answer is contained in the question. "How," he said, "can the Messiah be the Son of David when David himself spoke of the Messiah as his Lord?" The answer is: Obviously, he cannot be David's son in the sense that he is dependent on David and must carry out, as an obedient offspring, the traditions of his father. What Jesus wants to communicate to his auditors is that the Messiah is not the servant of Judaism. He did not come to deliver Israel on Israel's own terms; he did not come to put down her enemies and to exalt her above other nations: the Messiah is the servant of God. To be sure, he serves and delivers God's people, but only on God's terms, not theirs. He has come to help peoples of all nations, all races, all classes, and all times.

Juxtaposed here is a statement cast in the form of a warning. Jesus tells the people to beware of the scribes. In observing their behavior the people are warned not to behave like them. They advertise themselves by the clothes they wear; they indulge in frequent and long prayers; yet, they take unfair advantage of other people. Jesus speaks of them "as devouring widows' homes." On any pretense they will make a long prayer. He is afraid of religious leaders who cultivate the friendship of helpless widows only to acquire their property and resources for their own use. (Even today, some clergy are quite adept at this: they get personally remembered in wills. Women to whom they mean a lot give them handsome gifts and sometimes even expensive property.) The scribes desired recognition, honors, and rewards. Jesus wanted his followers to seek opportunities for service and to choose the privilege of giving, not receiving, that they might be the benefactors rather than the beneficiaries of all.

The last incident in chapter twelve is a gem. Jesus calls his disciples' attention to a person who is the example of what he means. The poor widow whom he observes putting her gift into the offering is the personification of charity and Christian benevolence. Mark says that Jesus sat outside the treasury and watched people as they put in their gifts. According to the Mishna, there were thirteen receptacles for making their deposits. They were constructed in the shape of a trumpet. One walked up and dropped what he wanted to give into the large open space at the top of the horn. It was funnelled on through the stem until it entered the treasury at the end. Some people brought large and expensive gifts. The widow brought only two of the smallest and least valuable of coins. They have been graphically translated in the King James version as "mites"—so tiny that one could hardly see them—yet, they were all she had. They were her living. Jesus said she gave the biggest gift, because she gave everything. The worth of a gift to God does not depend on its material value. Its worth is calculated solely on its value to the person who gives it. It must cost the giver something. Its value lies in how big a sacrifice it is to him who makes it.


## THE GREAT WARNING
### (Chapter 13)

The prophetic ministry of Jesus ends with a solemn warning to his followers, in the form of a prediction of the future. This is known generally as "the little apocalypse." Some think that it has all the signs of apocalyptic utterances, so that it gathers up into one small piece the varieties and forms of apocalypticism and offers us an authentic example of this type of literature.

The word *apocalyptic* means "uncovered" or "revealed." Something hidden is brought to light. Moving shapes or shadows in the darkness suddenly stand forth, and we can see their exact form and appearance. People dream dreams and see visions. The precise meaning of these dreams and visions is disclosed to them by divine aid. It is like finding something overlaid with a heavy covering, so that it is a complete mystery, and then pulling back the covering and seeing exactly what it is. The classic example of apocalypticism is the second half of the book of Daniel. Daniel has a series of dreams, each one of which, when interpreted, gives an exact prediction of certain future events. This is what the thirteenth chapter of Mark does, too.

Commentators have said that this chapter contains the only single lengthy discourse of Jesus that is recorded in the Gospels. That is, perhaps, too sweeping a judgment. It presupposes that the Sermon on the Mount (much longer), in Saint Matthew, was either a compilation of sayings given at various times and places in Jesus' ministry and put together artificially by the evangelist in its present form, or else that it was a running commentary on many unrelated topics, without a single, clearly defined theme, so that it cannot be thought of as one discourse. Also, it neglects to take into account the discourses in Saint John's Gospel. All that can be said is that it is Jesus' longest apocalyptic discourse.

It is Mark's equivalent to the talks which John records that Jesus gave after the Last Supper. Antiquity expected its great personages to give advice and to make predictions on the eve of their death. What was said then was like a will, or last testament. The Old Testament accounts of Jacob and Moses, and Samuel and David illustrate the practice. We should expect Jesus to do the same thing.

Professor C. H. Dodd shies away from the word *apocalyptic.* He prefers to call this speech the warning speech of Jesus to his followers. He must admit, however, that it is couched in apocalyptic terms. It is better for us to consider it as Jesus' great warning to his church and to his people. It had to deal with the future, for the church had not yet come into existence, and his people, except for a bare nucleus, had not even been formed. He knew that his days on earth were nearing an end. He had to get his disciples ready for what would come upon him, and he had to prepare his church for all eventualities.

There is in the discourse, however, a dichotomy of which we must be aware, if we are to understand it at all. It deals with two different things: it is both specific and general. It is specific in that it refers to one definite incident which will take place in the immediate future, namely, the fall of Jerusalem in A.D. 70 (and perhaps, also, to its later destruction in A.D. 132). It also refers to the end of the world—and these references are general. There are signs of upheaval and confusion and destruction that will take place, perhaps intermittently and over long intervals before the end comes.

The fall of Jerusalem will be accompanied by the profanation of the Temple and of the city (Mark 13:14). People in Judea shall flee to the mountains (Mark 13:14b); people who are on top of houses should not come down (Mark 13:15); people who are working in the fields should not go back into the house to collect their clothes (Mark 13:15-16); and it will be dangerous for women who are pregnant or who have small children (Mark 13:17). Just pray God that this will not happen during the winter season (Mark 13:18). Fortunately, this wanton destruction will not last long. God will shorten it for the sake of his elect (Mark 12:20). While it does last, however, it will be the worst disaster since the flood (Mark 13:19). Many people will mistake this for the end of the world, and there will be many false prophets who will claim to be Christ. But be on guard not to believe any of them (Mark 13:21-22).

The end of the world, with its accompanying signs, follows this description of the fall of Jerusalem. It will

102

be cataclysmic. The sun will not shine and the moon will not have any light to reflect. Even the stars will fall out of their places in the heavens. The angels shall come and gather up God's elect in all parts of the earth, and the Son of Man will be seen riding on the clouds in glory (Mark 13:24-27).

Jesus tells his disciples how to behave in preparation for the fall of Jerusalem, and how to behave afterwards. When they are persecuted and brought before the magistrates, they are to depend on the Holy Ghost for what they are to say. This is applicable to all followers under all adverse conditions. It is applicable, therefore, for us now, whatever the circumstances in which we live. Nations are still rising up against nations, and there are still earthquakes and famines and troubles.

There is no profit to anybody in trying to predict "the eschaton," the coming of the end. No one knows—not even the Son himself—only the Father. All we are to do is to make sure that we are in a state of readiness. The "little apocalypse" ends with the admonition, "And what I say unto you, I say unto all, Watch" (Mark 13:37).

CHAPTER FOUR
## PERSONAL REFLECTION

1. You have heard the account of Palm Sunday and the events before the crucifixion numerous times. After reading them again, try to verbalize the significance these events hold in your own faith and witness.

2. Read and meditate on Mark 11:12-26. What does God's judgment mean in your life? Can you view God as both judging and loving? Why?

3. In our present-day mechanized world, how are you reminded that God is the creator?

4. Reflect upon what it means to prepare for the future. What does this preparation mean for you personally?

### CHAPTER FIVE

# SUFFERING SERVANT AND RISEN LORD
## (Mark 14–16)

### ADORATION AND TREACHERY
#### (14:1-11)

As "rivers reach their mightiest measure at the margin of the sea," so Mark's Gospel is most forceful at the cross and the empty tomb. Saint Mark is more at ease in the handling of his material in these last three chapters than he has been in the earlier ones. The stories, the anecdotes, and the sayings of Jesus were often repeated in the preaching that Mark heard. If this material came from those sermons, it becomes evident to us that his emphases reflect their central themes. It is equally evident that the heart and core of those sermons was the death and resurrection of Jesus and that the narration of those two events mainly constitutes the proclamation of the gospel by those earliest Christians. The cornerstone of Christianity was the death and resurrection of Jesus.

If Mark himself had a direct hand in the collection and arrangement of the material, it meant that he was much more familiar with the last of Jesus' career than he was with the first. Born and reared in Jerusalem, Mark possibly had little disposition to visit the countryside. He may have never gone into Galilee during Jesus' ministry there. We know that he was in Jerusalem, on hand for the events of the Passion.

Mark's account is so arranged that it reaches its climax in the Passion. He tells his story in such a way that everything in it depends on the Passion and, therefore, leads up to it. Jesus' three predictions of the Passion, which he made before he reached Jerusalem, are like the tolling of a great bell, the tones of which reach every niche and corner of the gospel.

The evangelist must give a reasonable explanation why Jesus was put to death as a criminal; otherwise, no one would be interested in his story. Dr. D. E. Nineham, a British exegete, put it graphically when he said that Jesus' conviction as a criminal in the Roman court was precisely the same as a conviction in London at Old Bailey today, where the chief witness for the prosecution would be the Archbishops of Canterbury and York. Therefore, Mark contends that it was at the heart of God's plan of redemption that his Son would come into the world and suffer and die for our sins. This was foretold by the prophets, so that the Old Testament itself gives validity to our Lord's passion and death. He was put to death by the Jews at the instigation of their leaders. Roman justice was subverted for political reasons and became injustice. The real criminal in the case was not Jesus but his prosecutors. God vindicated Jesus by raising him from the dead. Mark's account of the Passion and Resurrection is set in a clear and definite theological perspective.

Because of this, many New Testament scholars contend that Mark's Gospel is really only the last three chapters, the story of the suffering death and resurrection of Jesus. They say that the other thirteen chapters are merely an introduction to the final three chapters. There is ample reason for this contention, but we need only to realize that the servant motif which runs through Mark is brought to fulfillment in this last section where Jesus is portrayed as the suffering servant and risen Lord.

Mark opens his account of the Passion with exquisite artistry. Once again, he uses his unique method of introducing the story with two events, one of which is sandwiched between the first and second parts of another event. The part that is inserted is an inspiring incident of adoration and love. The other part is a plot of treachery and violence as black and contemptible as an act of betrayal could possibly be.

The leadership of Israel determines that Jesus must die. Yet, they think that it would not be wise during the Feast of the Passover. Too many people would be in town. His arrest might cause an uproar. Judas, one of the Twelve, decides to aid the leadership. He takes the initiative and goes to them—they do not come to him. But they are willing to pay him. He goes back and tries to ferret out the easiest way to carry out his nefarious scheme. Even in an act of betrayal, he does not want any inconvenience.

The lovely event that is inserted in this ugly and repulsive transaction took place at Bethany where Jesus spent his nights during Holy Week prior to his arrest. While he was taking dinner at the home of Simon the Leper, a woman came into the house with an alabaster container of expensive ointment. It was the custom of the wealthy to rub themselves with various fine oils, especially at feasts and special occasions. Presumably, what the woman brought was "nard," an import from India, expensive, and considered a luxury in the ancient world. That it came in an alabaster container indicates its value.

Ungents of this type were also used at burials. On such occasions the broken jar was generally left in pieces on the embalmed body in the grave. Jesus has this custom in mind when he says that the woman performed this beautiful act in anticipation of his burial. She paid him a tribute that people usually reserve for the dead, and she did so while he was yet alive. And he is grateful.

Some of his followers, in contrast, are critical. Why should such expensive ointment be wasted? Its sweet odors will last only for the evening. Jesus is not accustomed to such treatment. This has never happened to him before. It will not happen again. The ointment should have been sold, and the proceeds given to the poor.

Jesus rebukes them: The poor are always on hand; people have opportunities at any time to help them. But Jesus will not always be with them. This woman chose to pay tribute to him. Wherever his gospel is preached across the centuries, this story will be told. It will stand as a memorial to her, to her generosity, her devotion, her adoration of the Master, and her unselfish love.

The needs of humanity, great as they are, are no substitute for devotion to God and our expression of that devotion in expensive acts of worship, praise, and thanksgiving. Beautiful churches, magnificent cathedrals, splendid pageants, all have their place in the total scheme of things, just as do acts of philanthropy, halfway houses, medical centers, relief stations, and all other means of serving the poor. Each complements and supports the other. It is a misconception that sets service in competition with worship or diminishes either to increase the other.

In tying treachery to adoration in this paradoxical pair of incidents by which he introduces the Passion, Mark displays at once its two essential elements: the recognition of Jesus as the Messiah by his adoring followers, and his mistreatment and condemnation by the general public, including even one of his intimates, because he does not give them what they think a messiah is sent to give. Wherever there is adoration, there is the possibility of treachery. One whom some envy enough to betray, others are bound to adore.

## THE LAST SUPPER
(14:12-31)

The Festival of the Unleavened Bread lasted for an entire week. Included in it was the Feast of the Passover, observed after sunset on the fifteenth of

Nisan. The fifteenth of Nisan was the date of the original Passover, described in the Book of Exodus. The angel of death passed over the homes of the Israelites with the blood sprinkled on their door-posts and settled on the homes of the Egyptians, slaying the first-born in every family. It was the blood of the sacrificial animal, eaten by the Hebrews at meal time, that had spared their homes of death.

Ever since, the Passover was a sacred holiday for the Jews. It was observed every year. The animal was obtained and killed on the fourteenth of Nisan and prepared for the feast on the opening of the fifteenth, which was eventide (sundown) of the same twenty-four hour span. A day for the Jews was always from sunset to sunset, not from midnight to midnight, as it is with us. The sacrificial animal was the lamb. An entire meal was prepared around it as the main course.

The meal was ceremonial, but it was also filling and nutritionally satisfying. It was like Thanksgiving or Christmas dinner for us. Nonetheless, the food was symbolic. The bread had no yeast in it. Unleavened bread symbolized the past misery of the Hebrew people who in their Egyptian bondage had had to make bricks without straw. The bitter herbs were a sign of that slavery, while the lamb was the symbol that God had spared them the fate he inflicted on Egypt.

On the fourteenth of Nisan, in the morning, Jesus sent two of the disciples to make ready the place where he would observe with them the Passover. They were those closest to him, his adopted family. In the streets of Jerusalem they would find a man with a pitcher of water. He would be easy to spot, since only the women carried water in that fashion on their heads. Men used big buckets, which they carried on their shoulders or hauled in a cart. Evidently, the owner of the house and his family would be expecting Jesus, for the upper room would be in readiness for him and his disciples. Even today in some parts of the East an upper room is reserved in homes for special guests and even for strangers. (I know, for I have slept in them in villages in Asia Minor.)

They came, Jesus with the Twelve, after sunset, and began the meal. At the very outset, our Lord said, "One of you which eateth with me shall betray me." Their answer—surprised and stunned as they were—is more explicit in the Greek than in the English. The King James translation reads that each one of them responded with the question, "Is it I? Is it I?" But the original Greek is much more emphatic. Their response was not a question but a protest: "Not I, Lord; no, not I!"

Yet Jesus insisted: "*It is* one of the twelve, that dippeth with me in the dish " (Mark 14:20).

This means that he made his prediction before the meal itself was formally begun. Before the blessing at Passover, a big dish of cooked fruits was served. The guests dipped bread into a common dish, and ate the fruit mix on bread as an appetizer, as you and I do potato chips and dip before some of our meals.

Jesus then said the Passover prayer. It no doubt went something like this: "Praised be thou, O Lord our God, King of the universe, who causest bread to come forth out of the earth." The disciples all said, "Amen." Then Jesus broke the bread and gave it to them. The eating of bread together symbolized the unity of fellowship, their oneness one to another. In the bonds of fellowship they could stand. Without it, one little piece was no more than a fragment of the loaf. It would quickly be blown into oblivion.

It was expected of the head of the family that he would give a brief homily on the meaning of the Passover as he distributed the food to those at the table. This Jesus did, and he likened the bread to his own body. By implication, he would be the Passover they would remember and celebrate in the future.

The wine was not drunk until the rest of the meal had been consumed. It came as a follow-up at the end, just as we serve a demitasse (coffee) after formal dinners today. It was after the supper that he poured the wine and gave it to them to drink and told them that this was his own blood. David and Jonathan in the Old Testament had sealed their friendship in blood. As the disciples drank the wine symbolizing Jesus' own blood poured out for them, they took into themselves the divine property of his everlasting life. Blood was the symbol of life.

The Passover meal ended with the singing of a hymn. Jesus and the disciples sang as they walked away from the house toward the Mount of Olives. On Passover night the people were supposed to sleep inside Jerusalem, but the Mount of Olives as far as Bethphage was considered within the city limits.

On the way over, Jesus predicted that his disciples

would be embarrassed by him. Peter swore that he would rather die first. Jesus then said that before the cock should crow twice, Peter would deny him thrice. Our Lord never identified his traitor, but he did identify the man who would deny him. Jesus was the very one who had confessed at Caesarea Philippi that Jesus was the Messiah.

## AGONY IN THE GARDEN
(12:12-52)

The company moved from the house of the Last Supper to the Garden of Gethsemane. The two places were evidently not far apart. This would place the upper room somewhere in the vicinity of the Temple. To this day, tourists are shown the traditional site; it is in this general region, located atop Mount Zion. Though none of the first-century buildings remain standing, and though the terrain today is much higher than it was in Jesus' day, because of the accumulation of the debris of centuries, still, the general geography of the city and region is the same. Tradition is probably correct in its general location of the upper room.

If so, the company crossed readily over the Kidron Valley to Gethsemane on the lower slopes of the Mount of Olives. There can be no doubt whatever about this place. The olive trees still grow, some from the seeds of those same trees under which Jesus prayed while his disciples slept. It was in the lower region of the Garden that Jesus left most of his

disciples and said to them, "Sit here, while I pray."
But he took with him further into the garden, Peter,
James, and John, his intimates, who understood him
better than the rest. He needed them more now than
ever. He was emotionally upset; his soul was
troubled within him. So he asked them to watch with
him, to support him in prayer. They were to be his
prayer partners for the night, not to pray with him,
but for him. He expected the three of them to pray
together in intercessory prayer.

Our Lord himself moved on beyond them. Alone,
he fell down, with his face to the ground, and cried
aloud, asking God to relieve him of the agony and
suffering of the present hour by letting him escape
his fate; yet he was submissive to God, and said,
"Not what I will, but what thou wilt" (Mark 14:36).
Only the prayers in which we submit our wills to the
will of God are effective prayers. If we persist in
trying to bend his will to ours, rather than our wills to
his, what begins as prayer ends in whimpering
idolatry.

When he needed them most, however, the
disciples failed him. They were incapable of
engaging in intercessory prayer. Three times he
came to them, and three times he found them fast
asleep. The weakness of the flesh overcame their
commitment to pray. They sincerely wanted to
support Jesus in prayer, but they were too weak.
Every time, they gave way to sleep. There is deep
pathos in Jesus' words to Peter: "Simon, are you
asleep? Could you not watch one hour?"

Jesus is now utterly alone. Who can describe his

loneliness? His experience now is one that no one else can share—no, not even his three closest friends, not even the sensitive and discerning Peter. Alone he stands, all alone. The English translation, "greatly distressed and troubled," does not convey the poignancy of the Greek original. Someone has said that the Greek gives the impression of "shuddering awe." The German Lohmeyer says, "The Greek words depict the greatest possible degree of infinite horror and suffering." When Jesus says that his soul is "sorrowful, even unto death," he means that he is almost dead because of his sorrow. He might well mean that death is more desirable than such sorrow and that he would prefer death to the grief and anxiety he now feels. What he means is, "I had rather be dead than go through with what I am going through now."

Dean Van Bogart Dunn of Methesco Theological School drew an unforgettable comparison and contrast between two vivid scenes. The one, of Jesus and his disciples in the storm on the Sea of Galilee, and the other, of the Master, with Peter, James, and John in the Garden of Gethsemane. The Dean said that Jesus was not afraid of physical danger, so he slept through the storm, though his disciples were terrified. But in the Garden, in the presence of evil, and faced with a spiritual crisis, Jesus was troubled, while his disciples fell asleep. We tend always to be disturbed by dangers that we can see; we need, however, the discernment of the Son of God to cause us to take alarm at dangers within the soul.

Judas, at the head of the band of soldiers (either

the Temple guard, or others whom the chief priest had deputized to arrest Jesus), came upon them while Jesus was still speaking to his disciples. Judas betrayed Jesus, identifying him to the soldiers with a kiss. An act of the deepest and most intimate affection was perverted into the most heinous deed of ignominy and shame: betrayal.

Judas's kiss was perhaps more than a mere means of identification, and it may have been something less than a sign of either hatred or disgust. It may be that he deliberately chose the kiss as the means of his betrayal. It was his farewell kiss, his saying goodbye to Jesus forever. No doubt he admired Jesus at first; he would not otherwise have become his follower. His initial admiration must certainly have led to affection and even to love. But Jesus disappointed him. He did not set up a kingdom. He did not give Judas what he had expected. This was his way of severing his relationship to Jesus and the others. Jesus, he thought, would sooner or later be arrested anyway. He did not want to suffer with him. If this was to be the end of Jesus' activity, he would at least protect himself. Yes, and he might as well get something out of it, too. He protected himself by betraying Jesus. Yes, and he got money for his betrayal. And his kiss said something, too: "I loved you once, but you disappointed me. It is all over now. And this says good-bye, the way I want to say it. I am turning you in because I do not feel that you are good for our people. I have not betrayed you. You betrayed us and all Israel with us."

Evidently, the others tried to put up a fight to save

SUFFERING SERVANT AND RISEN LORD

Jesus. At least one of the disciples cut off the ear of a servant of the high priest. Jesus rebuked them all. He said, "Why have you come after me with arms, as if I were a brigand, a man of violence, a common criminal? I taught peacefully in the Temple. You could have arrested me there. I would not have put up any opposition. But you have come with swords and clubs in the night!"

His followers, including the disciples, now fled. There was a young man among them who had nothing on his body but a linen cloth. The soldiers tried to seize him. He left his cloth in their hands and ran away. Could that young man have been Mark, who wrote this Gospel?

## THE SANHEDRIN
### (14:53-72)

Christ was arraigned before the Sanhedrin. The scribes and chief priests and other religious leaders—the very persons who effected Jesus' arrest—became also his judges. He who was accused was tried by his accusers.

Moreover, this took place on the very night of the Passover. Mark himself had said this could not happen (Mark 14:2). It was unthinkable that the Sanhedrin would desecrate the Feast of the Passover by even meeting on that day, much less by hearing a criminal case. As Christmas is to us, when we eat at home with the family, so is Passover to the Jew. On that day a Jew stays in his own home and eats the

117

Passover ram with his wife and children, his grandchildren, and other close relatives. Did not God command, on peril of their lives, the children of Israel to stay safely at home on that horrible night when he passed over Egypt, slaying the first-born of the Egyptians, but sparing the Hebrews?

Some people have doubted the historicity of Mark's account of Jesus' trial, because he sets it on the night of the Passover. They call attention to the fact that in doing this he contradicts what he wrote earlier, namely, that the chief priests determined not to arrest Jesus during the feast. But this, in my mind, helps to establish the accuracy of Mark's Gospel. After all, he was fully aware of what he had written. All he had to do was erase his first statement to make it conform to the account of the trial. That he did not do so is evidence of his trustworthiness. To be sure, says Mark, the chief priests had no intention of trying Jesus on the night of the Passover, but they did. Circumstances altered their original intention; they changed their minds.

Now this is revealed in the way they did it. They finished the Passover meal first, just as did Jesus with his disciples. Then they convened—not in their formal meeting place, in the Temple precincts, but at the residence of the high priest himself. This was an emergency. This was an extraordinary session. They met informally to do formal business. This is what Mark intends to convey in his account. This is what he does convey. Let us more accurately call this a preliminary hearing rather than a formal trial.

First, he makes it convincingly clear that Jesus was

absolutely innocent. The charges were trumped-up charges. The witnesses did not agree among themselves. Secondly, the trial came about through the machinations of the Jewish religious leadership. The nation of Israel was not prepared to receive its Messiah; consequently, the open confession by Jesus of his messiahship is what put him to death. When he claimed to be the "Son of the Blessed," the high priest said, "We do not need any more evidence. The man has condemned himself." The Jewishness of Mark's account is unmistakable. The high priest does not call the name of God. He indulges in circumlocution to avoid naming God's name. The name of God was too sacred to be uttered by a pious Jew. But the high priest was quite content to have a creature of God who had done no harm put to death. He rent his garments in horror at what he called Jesus' blasphemy, yet he cried out for a fellow human-being's blood. Mark tells that the members of the Sanhedrin and their servants began to spit on Jesus. They struck him and otherwise abused him, as a result of his confession that he was the Messiah.

Outside the house of the high priest, another drama of the highest intensity was being enacted. While Jesus was being condemned by the Sanhe-drin, his enemies, he was being denied by the chief of the disciples, Peter, his friend. Humanly speaking, he had understanding and support at this time from nobody. The spiritual loneliness he felt in the Garden of Gethsemane, still unrelieved, was compounded by physical loneliness as well. His entire company had fled. Peter alone was left. He did have the hardihood to follow his Master, though at a safe distance. Now, however, under scrutiny, when the maid asked, "Are you not one of his company?" he denied that he even knew Jesus. Her insistent questioning was matched by his vehemence, until finally he denied Jesus with an oath. As he denied him for the third time, the cock crowed for the second time. The Master had said at the Last Supper, "Before the cock crow twice, thou shalt deny me thrice" (Mark 14:30).

Mark conveys in this story of the investigation by the Sanhedrin and the accounts of Peter's denial the utter rejection of Jesus by all parties involved. The messiahship, discovered and confessed by Peter so convincingly at Caesarea Philippi, and gladly acknowledged by the other eleven disciples, was entirely forgotten by all of them on the night of Jesus' arrest. Peter denied him; the others fled, like sheep without a shepherd.

## THE CRUCIFIXION
(Chapter 15)

Indeed, at Pilate's court and at the crucifixion, in Mark's account, the twelve disciples are conspicuous by their absence.

Friday morning, after the Sanhedrin met and ratified formally what its members had done informally at the high priest's house the night before, Jesus was carried before Pilate. Mark's rendition of the trial in the Roman Court indicates that it was really no trial at all. We do not learn anything from it about Roman jurisprudence or the particulars in this case. The conclusion of the Jewish trial and the piece of evidence that condemned Jesus is not raised here at all. He is indicted for being *the King of the Jews.* The reason he is so indicted is that he had to be accused of something that the Romans would deem dangerous to the state, a threat to law and order. Pilate does not take the accusation seriously. According to Mark, he never pronounces sentence. All he does is to trade him for Barabbas and to allow Barabbas's sentence of execution to be placed on Jesus while he sets Barabbas free.

All this would be puzzling to the degree of mystification and utter bewilderment unless we knew clearly from Mark's general approach the theological motive that led him to select and emphasize the particular facts of the case he presents. All he wants to do is convince his readers that the Jews rejected the very Messiah whom their own prophets had foretold. It was their sins that put Jesus to death. Pilate and the Romans were merely their tools. Most important of all was that in substituting Jesus for Barabbas, Pilate anticipates the action of God Almighty himself, when he substituted his own Son for us and allowed Jesus to die for our sins on the cross. The suffering servant of Isaiah came to full realization in Jesus of Nazareth. He is given the sentence of the murderous Barabbas and is sent to die in Barabbas' place on the cross. This is the full impact of Mark's account of Jesus' trial by Pilate (Mark 15:1-15). To the uninitiated, it is confusing, because it is so short. When we grasp

121

Mark's motive, we realize that he has said all that he needs to say.

The mockery by the soldiers is all of the same piece. In derision they crown Jesus with a crown of thorns. (This is not new. Jews made fun of Agrippa when Caligula made him king. When he reached Alexandria in Egypt, the Jewish residents picked up a half-wit, put a paper crown on his head, and called him Agrippa. When Agrippa entered the city and saw his demented rival, he realized how the people of his own race despised him because of what the Roman Empire had done for him.) The soldiers beat Jesus with whips and lacerated his body with the metal rods imbedded in the cords of the whips. Was not the suffering servant of the Lord to be wounded for our transgressions and bruised for our iniquity? (Isaiah 53:5) The soldiers tapped him on the head with a reed, as if they were anointing him. They bowed before him and laughed and jested at him. They spat in his face (Mark 15:16-20).

Mark is sparing in his narrative of the crucifixion. He tells us so little that it is exasperating. Yet he tells us what he thinks we need to know to understand his message. Jesus is not physically strong enough to carry his own cross. A stranger is impressed to carry the cross for him. The stranger is not a native Jew; he is a Cyrenian, a Jew of the Dispersion, who has come back to Jerusalem for the Feast. His sons are Alexander and Rufus. That is all Mark says about him; but Simon of Cyrene evidently became a Christian, and his two sons are so prominent in the Roman Church that they need no identification. What a moving lesson in evangelization! By just the carrying of Jesus' cross—and that, no doubt, against his will—an utter stranger is converted. The gospel is for everybody, and it compels our allegiance most when it takes the shape of a cross.

In death, even a criminal evokes acts of pity and compassion. Jesus is thought to be a criminal, for he is crucified between two thieves. There are some in the mocking crowd who extend to him wine mingled with myrrh, a drink that relieves pain. He refuses it. He wants to be mentally alert to the end.

He is mocked and derided in his misery. His own teachings are used against him: "If you can destroy and rebuild the Temple, why can't you save yourself? How can you help us if you can't help yourself?" Many who had listened to him earlier now ridicule and despise him.

Even Jesus breaks under the strain. He calls out as if God had forgotten him: "Why hast thou forsaken me?" (Mark 15:34). This was misunderstood by the reviling mob. It is the first verse of Psalm 22. Perhaps Jesus was quoting the entire psalm, and the mob heard only the first verse. The psalm in its entirety is a psalm of praise and triumph: "For he hath not despised nor abhorred the affliction of the afflicted; neither hath he hid his face from him; but when he cried unto him, he heard" (Psalm 22:24). Certainly they misunderstood, for they thought that he called for Elijah to help him, and Elijah did not come.

Only the women were at the cross. One of them was Mary Magdalene, whom Jesus had saved. This converted sinner remained faithful to the end. It was

123

she and the other Mary who observed precisely the tomb in which Jesus' body was laid.

God demonstrated his power. The veil of the Temple was rent in two. No longer could the Jews be isolated religiously. No longer could they claim to be God's chosen people. The Holy of holies, reserved only for the high priest once a year, on the Day of Atonement, was now revealed to everybody. And the centurion was converted: a Roman soldier became a Christian on the day of the crucifixion. The benefits of the cross were for the gentiles, for all people.

Even a member of the Sanhedrin, Joseph of Arimathea, gave Jesus his tomb. At least some of those who condemned Jesus confessed their mistake and sought to honor him. The Romans customarily left crucified bodies to rot on the cross, but sometimes they permitted families to take them down for burial. This permission was granted by Pilate.

Mark tells the story of the crucifixion to portray the universal nature of redemption and the efficacy of the cross for everybody; the grateful followers, such as Mary Magdalene; the repentant Jewish judge, Joseph of Arimathea; and the gentile soldier and executioner, the Roman centurian. Truly, this innocent man died for our sins—and because of him we are saved.

## THE RESURRECTION
(Chapter 16)

Jesus was the authentic revelation of the nature and character of God. He was the servant of the Lord, the messianic servant, the prophetic servant, and, finally, the suffering servant. His crucifixion authentically revealed the form of God's mission for the redemption of his people, through his resurrection from the dead. He, whom Mark has presented all through his gospel as servant, is now shown to be the Lord. The climax of the gospel is the resurrection. This is the glorious end toward which Mark's Gospel moves from the beginning.

The sombre sadness of chapters fourteen and fifteen is relieved, indeed completely dissipated, in chapter sixteen. The long night that envelopes the events of Friday, that holds a deathly stillness throughout Saturday, is penetrated by a shaft of light early on Sunday morning and is broken entirely by sunshine as the day progresses.

Perhaps Mark's story appropriately ends with verse eight of chapter sixteen. The two oldest Greek manuscripts contain no more than these few verses. Eusebius, the first great church historian, and Saint Jerome, the greatest biblical scholar of antiquity, both of whom lived in the fourth century, testify that the best Greek manuscripts they know end with the eighth verse. Yet Irenaeus, who lived earlier in the second century, knew and accepted these additional verses. The point is purely academic, for the account of the resurrection is given in the first eight verses; the remaining verses only confirm and amplify that testimony.

The two Marys, who observed where Jesus had been buried, went at daylight on Sunday to his tomb. They wanted to anoint his body with spices, which they had not been able to do on Friday afternoon due to the fast approaching sabbath. They had a problem. They did not know where they could find strong men to roll back the stone for them so they could enter the tomb. It was customary in those days for Jews to visit each morning the grave of a loved one for three successive days after burial.

The stone was rolled back. A young man in white sat inside the tomb. He was, no doubt, an angel who in appearance and speech had accommodated himself to the needs of the women who were unfamiliar with the sights and sounds of heaven. It was he who told them that Jesus was risen from the dead, the very news of which filled them with awesome fear. "The one who was so familiar to you and was always with you was in reality the Son of God." This news was more than they could take at the time. So ends verse eight.

Verse nine begins what is almost an entirely different story. The transition is abrupt. The writer tells us simply that Jesus appeared to Mary Magdalene and to two other people in the country, as they were walking together; and they came and told the disciples, but nobody believed them. Later, however, Jesus appeared to the eleven as they sat eating a meal, and he rebuked them because they had not believed Mary Magdalene and the two persons from the country. Then, he commissioned the eleven "to preach the gospel to every creature." He told them that those who believed and accepted baptism would be saved. Those who did not would be damned. Likewise, he promised them signs in the